Transformation and Healing

Sutra on the Four Establishments of Mindfulness

THICH NHAT HANH

16pt

Copyright Page from the Original Book

Parallax Press
P.O. Box 7355
Berkeley, California 94707
www.parallax.org

Parallax Press is the publishing division of Unified Buddhist Church, Inc.

This edition copyright © 2006 by Unified Buddhist Church.
All Rights Reserved.
Printed in Canada on 100% recycled paper.
Distributed by Publishers Group West.

No part of this book may be reproduced in any form or by any means, electronic or mechanical, including photocopying, recording, or by any other information storage and retrieval system or technologies now known or later developed, without permission in writing from the publisher.

Sutra translated from the Pali by Thich Nhat Hanh and Annabel Laity.
Translated from the Vietnamese by Annabel Laity.

Cover design by Charles Woods.
Text design by Dennis Crean.

Library of Congress Cataloging-in-Publication Data

[Insert CIP data here]

1 2 3 4 5 / 10 09 08 07 06

TABLE OF CONTENTS

A NOTE ON THE TEXT	i
Introduction: What Is Mindfulness?	ii
Sutra on the Four Establishments of Mindfulness	1
Summary of the Sutra	25
Mindfulness Exercises	28
Principles for the Practice of Mindfulness	127
Conclusion	143
Appendix: Three Versions of the Sutra	146
Back Cover Material	192

A NOTE ON THE TEXT

The word for a Buddhist scripture, the teachings of the Buddha, is *sutta* in Pali and *sutra* in Sanskrit. Because a number of texts, Pali, Sanskrit, and Chinese, are cited throughout the commentary, we use the word *sutra* as if it were an English word and use the word *sutta* only when it is part of the proper name of a Pali sutta, such as Satipatthana Sutta or Anapanasati Sutta.

The word *satipatthana* (Sanskrit: *smrityupasthana*) is a compound of *sati*, which means "mindfulness" or "remembering," and *upatthana*, which means "place of abiding," "establishment," or "application." In Chinese, the title of the sutra is Nian Chu. *Nian* is "to be mindful of," "to put one's attention to," or "to remember." *Chu* means either "the dwelling place" or "the act of dwelling," "the act of being present," "the act of establishing oneself." Nian Chu therefore may be translated as "the Four Grounds of Mindfulness" or "the Four Establishments of Mindfulness."

For ease of use, the text of the original sutra has been kept with the male pronouns, *he* and *his*, throughout, although clearly the message is intended for practitioners of any gender. This was done for ease of reading and to keep as close to the original as possible.

Introduction: What Is Mindfulness?

We practice mindfulness in order to realize liberation, peace, and joy in our everyday lives. Liberation and happiness are linked to each other; if there is liberation, there is happiness, and greater liberation brings greater happiness. If there is liberation, peace and joy exist in the present moment. We don't need to wait ten or fifteen years to realize them. They're available as soon as we begin the practice. However modest these elements may be, they form the basis for greater liberation, peace, and joy in the future.

To practice meditation is to look deeply in order to see into the essence of things. With insight and understanding we can realize liberation, peace, and joy. Our anger, anxiety, and fear are the ropes that bind us to suffering. If we want to be liberated from them, we need to observe their nature, which is ignorance, the lack of clear understanding. When we misunderstand a friend, we may become angry at him, and because of that, we may suffer. But when we look deeply into what has happened, we can end the misunderstanding. When we understand the other person and his situation, our suffering will disappear and peace and joy will arise. The first step is awareness of the object, and the second step is looking deeply at the object to shed light on it. Therefore, mindfulness means awareness and it also means looking deeply.

The Pali word *sati* (Sanskrit: *smrti*) means "to stop," and "to maintain awareness of the object." The Pali word *vipassana* (Sanskrit: *vipashyana*) means "to go deeply into that object to observe it." While we are fully aware of and observing deeply an object, the boundary between the subject who observes and the object being observed gradually dissolves, and the subject and object become one. This is the essence of meditation. Only when we penetrate an object and become one with it can we understand. It is not enough to stand outside and observe an object. That's why the Sutra on the Four Establishments of Mindfulness reminds us to be aware of the body in the body, the feelings in the feelings, the mind in the mind, and the objects of mind in the objects of mind.

The Buddha delivered the Sutra on the Four Establishments of Mindfulness to an audience of monks and nuns, *bhikkhus* and *bhikkhunis*. But that doesn't mean that the practice of being mindful in the ground of the Four Establishments is limited to monks and nuns. Anyone can practice mindfulness. If monks and nuns can practice mindfulness in walking, standing, lying down, and sitting, then laymen and laywomen also can. Is there anyone who does not walk, stand, lie down, and sit every day? What is most important is to understand the fundamental basis of the practice and then apply it during our everyday lives, even if our lives are different from the way the Buddha and his monks and nuns lived twenty-five centuries ago. When reading the Sutra on the Four Establishments of Mindfulness, we have to read with the eyes of a person of today and discover appropriate ways to practice based on the teachings of the sutra.[1]

Mindfulness is always mindfulness of something. There are four areas of mindfulness, four areas where mindfulness has to penetrate in order for us to be protected, for joy to be nourished, for pain to be transformed, and for insight to be obtained. These are called the Four Establishments of Mindfulness. These four establishments, or foundations, are body, feelings, mind, and objects of mind.

The First Establishment of Mindfulness is mindfulness of the body in the body. This means that when you bring mindfulness into your body, mindfulness becomes the body. Mindfulness is not an outside observer. Mindfulness becomes the body, and the body becomes mindfulness.

---

[1] To understand the Sutra on the Four Establishments of Mindfulness more deeply, readers are advised to study the Sutra on the Full Awareness of Breathing, see Thich Nhat Hanh, Breathe! You Are Alive (Berkeley, CA: Parallax Press, 1996); and the Sutra on the Better Way to Live Alone, see Thich Nhat Hanh, Our Appointment with Life (Berkeley, CA: Parallax Press, 1990).

When mother embraces child, mother becomes child, and child becomes mother. In true meditation, the subject and the object of meditation no longer exist as separate entities; that distinction is removed. When you generate the energy of mindfulness and embrace your breathing and your body, that is mindfulness of the body in the body. Mindfulness is not an outside observer, it *is* the body. The body becomes the object and the subject of mindfulness at the same time.

It's like when nuclear scientists say that to understand an elementary particle and really enter into the world of the infinitely small, you have to become a participant and not an observer anymore. In India they use the example of a grain of salt that would like to know how salty the ocean is. How can a grain of salt come to know this? The only way is for it to jump into the ocean, and the understanding will be perfect; the separation between the object of understanding and the subject of understanding is no longer there. In our time, nuclear scientists have begun to see that. That is why they say that in order to really understand the world of the elementary particle, you have to stop being an observer, you have to become a participant.

The Second Establishment of Mindfulness is our feelings. The Third Establishment of Mindfulness is the mind, namely the mental formations. In the Sutra on the Full Awareness of Breathing, the Buddha offered us four exercises of mindful breathing to take care of each of these fields of our mindfulness.

The Fourth Establishment of Mindfulness is the realm of perception. In the sutra it is spoken of as "the objects of mind," and we can understand this as perception. The Buddha also proposed four exercises on mindful breathing for contemplation of the objects of mind in the objects of mind, so that we can penetrate, embrace, and look deeply into the object of our perception. Doing so gives us the insight that will liberate us from our delusion and our suffering.

Mountains, rivers, birds, the blue sky, houses, streams, children, animals—everything is the object of your perception. And we have four exercises of mindful breathing in order to help us inquire about the true nature of all these things, including ourselves. Body is also an object of mind, feelings are also objects of our mind, and mental formations become objects of our mind. We can always inquire about the nature of our body, our feelings, or our mind, as well as our perceptions and other things. If we look deeply at the body in the body, it becomes an object of the mind. When we are looking at feelings, then feelings are the object of mind. When we are observing mind, mind becomes the object of our mind. All the establishments of mindfulness are in fact objects of mind.

A monk once asked me how mind can be an object of mind. I said if we take our two fingers and rub them together, then the body is in touch with the body. The mind is the same. When we look into our body, our body is the object of our mind. When we look into form, form is the object of our mind. When we look into mental formations, mental formations are the object of our mind. So we see that the field of objects of mind is very vast. But the division into four establishments is a convenient tool to help us learn how to practice mindfulness.

If you would like to study meditation, this Sutra on the Four Establishments of Mindfulness is part of your foundation. This is one of the sutras you keep under your pillow, always with you.

Sutra on the Four Establishments of Mindfulness

Satipatthana Sutta (Theravada) from Majjhima Nikaya, 10.

I.

I heard these words of the Buddha one time when he was living at Kammassadharma, a market town of the Kuru people. The Buddha addressed the bhikkhus, "O bhikkhus."

And the bhikkhus replied, "Venerable Lord."

The Buddha said, "Bhikkhus, there is a most wonderful way to help living beings realize purification, overcome directly grief and sorrow, end pain and anxiety, travel the right path, and realize nirvana. This way is the Four Establishments of Mindfulness.

"What are the Four Establishments?

1. "Bhikkhus, a practitioner remains established in the observation of the body in the body, diligent, with clear understanding, mindful, having abandoned every craving and every distaste for this life.

2. "He remains established in the observation of the feelings in the feelings, diligent, with clear understanding, mindful, having abandoned every craving and every distaste for this life.
3. "He remains established in the observation of the mind in the mind, diligent, with clear understanding, mindful, having abandoned every craving and every distaste for this life.
4. "He remains established in the observation of the objects of mind in the objects of mind, diligent, with clear understanding, mindful, having abandoned every craving and every distaste for this life."

II.

"And how does a practitioner remain established in the observation of the body in the body?

"He goes to the forest, to the foot of a tree, or to an empty room, sits down cross-legged in the lotus position, holds his body straight, and establishes mindfulness in front of him. He breathes in, aware that he is breathing in. He breathes out, aware that he is breathing out. When he breathes in a long breath, he knows, 'I am breathing in a long breath.' When he breathes out a long breath, he knows, 'I am breathing out a long breath.' When he breathes in a short breath, he knows, 'I am breathing in a short breath.' When he breathes out a short breath, he knows, 'I am breathing out a short breath.'

"He uses the following practice: 'Breathing in, I am aware of my whole body. Breathing out, I am aware of my whole body.' And then, 'Breathing in, I calm my body. Breathing out, I calm my body.'

"Just as a skilled turner knows when he makes a long turn, 'I am making a long turn,' and knows when he makes a short turn, 'I am making a short turn,' so a practitioner, when he breathes in a long breath, knows, 'I am breathing in a long breath,' and when he breathes in a short breath knows, 'I am breathing in a short breath,' when he breathes out a long breath, knows, 'I am breathing out a long breath,' and when he breathes out a short breath knows, 'I am breathing out a short breath.'

"He uses the following practice: 'Breathing in, I am aware of my whole body. Breathing out, I am aware of my whole body. Breathing in, I calm my body. Breathing out, I calm my body.'

"This is how a practitioner observes the body in the body. He observes the body from within or from without, or from both within and without. He observes the process of coming-to-be in the body or the process of dissolution in the body or both the process of coming-to-be and the process of dissolution. Or he is mindful of the fact, 'There is a body here,' until understanding and full awareness come about. He maintains the observation, free, not caught up in any worldly consideration. That is how to practice observation of the body in the body, O bhikkhus.

"Moreover, when a practitioner walks, he is aware, 'I am walking.' When he is standing, he is aware, 'I am standing.' When he is sitting, he is aware, 'I am sitting.' When he is lying down, he is aware, 'I am lying down.' In whatever position his body happens to be, he is aware of the position of his body.

"This is how a practitioner observes the body in the body. He observes the body from within or from without, or from both within and without. He observes the process of coming-to-be in the body or the process of dissolution in the body or both the process of coming-to-be and the process of dissolution. Or he is mindful of the fact, 'There is a body here,' until understanding and full awareness come about. He maintains the observation, free, not caught up in any worldly consideration. That is how to practice observation of the body in the body, O bhikkhus.

"Moreover, when the practitioner is going forward or backward, he applies full awareness to his going forward or backward. When he looks in front or looks behind, bends down or stands up, he also applies full awareness to what he is doing. He applies full awareness to wearing the sanghati robe or carrying the alms bowl. When he eats or drinks, chews or savors the food, he applies full awareness to all this. When passing excrement or urinating, he applies full awareness to this. When he walks, stands, lies down, sits, sleeps or wakes up, speaks or is silent, he shines his awareness on all this.

"Further, the practitioner meditates on his very own body from the soles of the feet upwards and then from the hair on top of the head downwards, a body contained inside the skin and full of all the impurities which belong to the body: 'Here is the hair of the head, the hairs on the body, the nails, teeth, skin, flesh, sinews, bones, bone marrow, kidneys, heart, liver, diaphragm, spleen, lungs, intestines, bowels, excrement, bile, phlegm, pus, blood, sweat, fat, tears, grease, saliva, mucus, synovic fluid, urine.'

"Bhikkhus, imagine a sack which can be opened at both ends, containing a variety of grains: brown rice, wild rice, mung beans, kidney beans, sesame seeds, white rice. When someone with good eyesight opens the bag, he will review it like this: 'This is brown rice, this is wild rice, these are mung beans, these are kidney beans, these are sesame seeds, this is white rice.' Just so the practitioner passes in review the whole of his body from the soles of the feet to the hair on the top of the head, a body enclosed in a layer of skin and full of all the impurities which belong to the body: 'Here is the hair of the head, the hairs on the body, nails, teeth, skin, flesh, sinews, bones, bone marrow, kidneys, heart, liver, diaphragm, spleen, lungs, intestines, bowels, excrement, bile, phlegm, pus, blood, sweat, fat, tears, grease, saliva, mucus, synovic fluid, urine.'

"This is how the practitioner remains established in the observation of the body in the body; observation of the body from within or from without, or from both within and without. He remains established in the observation of the process of coming-to-be in the body or the process of dissolution in the body or both the process of coming-to-be and the process of dissolution. Or he is mindful of the fact, 'There is a body here,' until understanding and full awareness come about. He remains established in the observation, free, not caught up in any worldly consideration. That is how to practice observation of the body in the body, O bhikkhus.

"Further, in whichever position his body happens to be, the practitioner passes in review the elements which constitute the body: 'In this body is the earth element, the water element, the fire element, and the air element.'

"As a skilled butcher or an apprentice butcher, having killed a cow, might sit at the crossroads to divide the cow into many parts, the practitioner passes in review the elements which comprise his very own body: 'Here in this body are the earth element, the water element, the fire element, and the air element.'

"This is how the practitioner remains established in the observation of the body in the body: observation of the body from within or from without, or from both within and without. He remains established in the observation of the process of coming-to-be in the body or the process of dissolution in the body or both the process of coming-to-be and the process of dissolution. Or he is mindful of the fact, 'There is a body here,' until understanding and full awareness come about. He remains established in the observation, free, not caught up in any worldly consideration. That is how to practice observation of the body in the body, O bhikkhus.

"Further, the practitioner compares his own body with a corpse which he imagines he sees thrown onto a charnel ground and lying there for one, two, or three days, bloated, blue in color, and festering, and he observes, 'This body of mine is of the same nature. It will end up in the same way; there is no way it can avoid that state.'

"This is how the practitioner remains established in the observation of the body in the body: observation of the body from within or from without, or from both within and without. He remains established in the observation of the process of coming-to-be in the body or the process of dissolution in the body or both the process of coming-to-be and the process of dissolution. Or he is mindful of the fact, 'There is a body here,' until understanding and full awareness come about. He remains established in the observation, free, not caught up in any worldly consideration. That is how to practice observation of the body in the body, O bhikkhus.

"Further, the practitioner compares his own body with a corpse which he imagines he sees thrown onto a charnel ground, pecked at by crows, eaten by hawks, vultures, and jackals, and infested with maggots and worms, and he observes, 'This body of mine is of the same nature, it will end up in the same way, there is no way it can avoid that state.'

"This is how the practitioner remains established in the observation of the body in the body; observation of the body from within or from without, or from both within and without. He remains established in the observation of the process of coming-to-be in the body or the process of dissolution in the body or both the process of coming-to-be and the process of dissolution. Or he is mindful of the fact, 'There is a body here,' until understanding and full awareness come about. He remains established in the observation, free, not caught up in any worldly consideration. That is how to practice observation of the body in the body, O bhikkhus.

"Further, the practitioner compares his own body with a corpse which he imagines he sees thrown onto a charnel ground; it is just a skeleton with a little flesh and blood sticking to it, and the bones are held together by the ligaments, and he observes, 'This body of mine is of the same nature. It will end up in the same way. There is no way it can avoid that state.'

"Further, the practitioner compares his own body with a corpse which he imagines he sees thrown onto a charnel ground; it is just a skeleton, no longer adhered to by any flesh, but still smeared by a little blood, the bones still held together by the ligaments...

"Further, the practitioner compares his own body with a corpse which he imagines he sees thrown onto a charnel ground; it is just a skeleton, no longer adhered to by any flesh nor smeared by any blood, but the bones are still held together by the ligaments...

"Further, the practitioner compares his own body with a corpse which he imagines he sees thrown onto a charnel ground; all that is left is a collection of bones scattered here and there; in one place a hand bone, in another a shin bone, a thigh bone, a pelvis, a spinal column, a skull...

"Further, the practitioner compares his own body with a corpse which he imagines he sees thrown onto a charnel ground; all that is left is a collection of bleached bones, the color of shells...

"Further, the practitioner compares his own body with a corpse which he imagines he sees thrown onto a charnel ground; it has been lying there for more than one year and all that is left is a collection of dried bones...

"Further, the practitioner compares his own body with a corpse which he imagines he sees thrown onto a charnel ground; all that is left is the dust which comes from the rotted bones and he observes, 'This body of mine is of the same nature, it will end up in the same way. There is no way it can avoid that state.'

"This is how the practitioner remains established in the observation of the body in the body, observation of the body from within or from without, or from both within and without. He remains established in the observation of the process of coming-to-be in the body or the process of dissolution in the body or both the process of coming-to-be and the process of dissolution. Or he is mindful of the fact, 'There is a body here,' until understanding and full awareness come about. He remains established in the observation, free, not caught up in any worldly consideration. That is how to practice observation of the body in the body, O bhikkhus."

III.

"Bhikkhus, how does a practitioner remain established in the observation of the feelings in the feelings?

"Whenever the practitioner has a pleasant feeling, he is aware, 'I am experiencing a pleasant feeling.' Whenever he has a painful feeling, he is aware, 'I am experiencing a painful feeling.' Whenever he experiences a feeling that is neither pleasant nor painful, he is aware, 'I am experiencing a neutral feeling.' When he experiences a pleasant feeling based in the body, he is aware, 'I am experiencing a pleasant feeling based in the body.' When he experiences a pleasant feeling based in the mind, he is aware, 'I am experiencing a pleasant feeling based in the mind.' When he experiences a painful feeling based in the body, he is aware, 'I am experiencing a painful feeling based in the body.' When he experiences a painful feeling based in the mind, he is aware, 'I am experiencing a painful feeling based in the mind.' When he experiences a neutral feeling based in the body, he is aware, 'I am experiencing a neutral feeling based in the body.' When he experiences a neutral feeling based in the mind, he is aware, 'I am experiencing a neutral feeling based in the mind.'

"This is how the practitioner remains established in the observation of the feelings in the feelings, observation of the feelings from within or from without, or observation of the feelings from both within and without. He remains established in the observation of the process of coming-to-be in the feelings or the process of dissolution in the feelings or both the process of coming-to-be and the process of dissolution. Or he is mindful of the fact, 'There is feeling here,' until understanding and full awareness come about. He remains established in the observation, free, not caught up in any worldly consideration. That is how to practice observation of the feelings in the feelings, O bhikkhus."

IV.

"Bhikkhus, how does a practitioner remain established in the observation of the mind in the mind?

"When his mind is desiring, the practitioner is aware, 'My mind is desiring.' When his mind is not desiring, he is aware, 'My mind is not desiring.' When his mind is hating something, he is aware, 'My mind is hating.' When his mind is not hating, he is aware, 'My mind is not hating.' When his mind is in a state of ignorance, he is aware, 'My mind is in a state of ignorance.' When his mind is not in a state of ignorance, he is aware, 'My mind is not in a state of ignorance.' When his mind is collected, he is aware, 'My mind is collected.' When his mind is not collected, he is aware, 'My mind is not collected.' When his mind is distracted, he is aware, 'My mind is distracted.' When his mind is not distracted, he is aware, 'My mind is not distracted.' When his mind has a wider scope, he is aware, 'My mind has widened in scope.' When his mind has a narrow scope, he is aware, 'My mind has become narrow in scope.' When his mind is capable of reaching a higher state, he is aware, 'My mind is capable of reaching a higher state.' When his mind is not capable of reaching a higher state, he is aware, 'My mind is not capable of reaching a higher state.' When his mind is composed, he is aware, 'My mind is composed.' When his mind is not composed, he is aware, 'My mind is not composed.' When his mind is free, he is aware, 'My mind is free.' When his mind is not free, he is aware, 'My mind is not free.'

"This is how the practitioner remains established in the observation of the mind in the mind, observation of the mind from within or from without, or observation of the mind from both within and without. He remains established in the observation of the process of coming-to-be in the mind or the process of dissolution in the mind or both the process of coming-to-be and the process of dissolution. Or he is mindful of the fact, 'There is mind here,' until understanding and full awareness come about. He remains established in the observation, free, not caught up in any worldly consideration. This is how to practice observation of the mind in the mind, O bhikkhus."

V.

"Bhikkhus, how does a practitioner remain established in the observation of the objects of mind in the objects of mind?

"First of all, he observes the objects of mind in the objects of mind with regard to the Five Hindrances. How does he observe this?

1. "When sensual desire is present in him, he is aware, 'Sensual desire is present in me.' Or when sensual desire is not present in him, he is aware, 'Sensual desire is not present in me.' When sensual desire begins to arise, he is aware of it. When already arisen sensual desire is abandoned, he is aware of it. When sensual desire already abandoned will not arise again in the future, he is aware of it.

2. "When anger is present in him, he is aware, 'Anger is present in me.' When anger is not present in him, he is aware, 'Anger is not present in me.' When anger begins to arise, he is aware of it. When already arisen anger is abandoned, he is aware of it. When anger already abandoned will not arise again in the future, he is aware of it.

3. "When dullness and drowsiness are present in him, he is aware, 'Dullness and drowsiness are present in me.' When dullness and drowsiness are not present in him, he is aware, 'Dullness and drowsiness are not present in me.' When dullness and drowsiness begin to arise, he is aware of it. When already arisen dullness and drowsiness are abandoned, he is aware of it. When dullness and drowsiness already

abandoned will not arise again in the future, he is aware of it.

4. "When agitation and remorse are present in him, he is aware, 'Agitation and remorse are present in me.' When agitation and remorse are not present in him, he is aware, 'Agitation and remorse are not present in me.' When agitation and remorse begin to arise, he is aware of it. When already arisen agitation and remorse are abandoned, he is aware of it. When agitation and remorse already abandoned will not arise again in the future, he is aware of it.

5. "When doubt is present in him, he is aware, 'Doubt is present in me.' When doubt is not present in him, he is aware, 'Doubt is not present in me.' When doubt begins to arise, he is aware of it. When already arisen doubt is abandoned, he is aware of it. When doubt already abandoned will not arise again in the future, he is aware of it.

"This is how the practitioner remains established in the observation of the objects of mind in the objects of mind: observation of the objects of mind from within or from without, or observation of the objects of mind from both within and without. He remains established in the observation of the process of coming-to-be in the objects of mind or the process of dissolution in the objects of mind or both the process of coming-to-be and the process of dissolution. Or he is mindful of the fact, 'There is an object of the mind here,' until understanding and full awareness come about. He remains established in the observation, free, not caught up in any worldly consideration. That is how to practice observation of the objects of mind in the objects of mind with regard to the Five Hindrances, O bhikkhus.

"Further, the practitioner observes the objects of mind in the objects of mind with regard to the Five Aggregates of Clinging. How does he observe this?

"He observes like this: 'Such is form. Such is the arising of form. Such is the disappearance of form. Such is feeling. Such is the arising of feeling. Such is the disappearance of feeling. Such is perception. Such is the arising of perception. Such is the disappearance of perception. Such are mental formations. Such is the arising of mental formations. Such is the disappearance of mental formations. Such is consciousness. Such is the arising of consciousness. Such is the disappearance of consciousness.'

"This is how the practitioner remains established in the observation of the objects of mind in the objects of mind with regard to the Five Aggregates of Clinging: observation of the objects of mind from within or from without, or observation of the objects of mind from both within and without. He remains established in the observation of the process of coming-to-be in the object of mind or the process of dissolution in the object of mind or both the process of coming-to-be and the process of dissolution. Or he is mindful of the fact, 'There is an object of mind here,' until understanding and full awareness come about. He remains established in the observation, free, not caught up in any worldly consideration. That is how to practice observation of the objects of mind in the objects of mind with regard to the Five Aggregates, O bhikkhus.

"Further, bhikkhus, the practitioner observes the objects of mind in the objects of mind with regard to the six sense organs and the six sense objects. How does he observe this?

"He is aware of the eyes and aware of the form, and he is aware of the internal formations which are produced in dependence on these two things. He is aware of the birth of a new internal formation and is aware of abandoning an already produced internal formation, and he is aware when an already abandoned internal formation will not arise again.

"The practitioner is aware of the ears and aware of the sound, and he is aware of the internal formations which are produced in dependence on these two things. He is aware of the birth of a new internal formation and is aware of abandoning an already produced internal formation, and he is aware when an already abandoned internal formation will not arise again.

"The practitioner is aware of the nose and aware of the smell, and he is aware of the internal formations which are produced in dependence on these two things. He is aware of the birth of a new internal formation and is aware of abandoning an already produced internal formation, and he is aware when an already abandoned internal formation will not arise again.

"The practitioner is aware of the tongue and aware of the taste, and he is aware of the internal formations which are produced in dependence on these two things. He is aware of the birth of a new internal formation and is aware of abandoning an already produced internal formation, and he is aware when an already abandoned internal formation will not arise again.

"The practitioner is aware of the body and aware of the object touched, and he is aware of the internal formations which are produced in dependence on these two things. He is aware of the birth of a new internal formation and is aware of abandoning an already produced internal formation, and he is aware when an already abandoned internal formation will not arise again.

"The practitioner is aware of the mind and aware of the objects of mind (the world), and he is aware of the internal formations which are produced in dependence on these two things. He is aware of the birth of a new internal formation and is aware of abandoning an already produced internal formation, and he is aware when an already abandoned internal formation will not arise again.

"This is how the practitioner remains established in the observation of the objects of mind in the objects of mind with regard to the six sense organs and the six sense objects: observation of the objects of mind from within or from without, or observation of the objects of mind from both within and without. He remains established in the observation of the process of coming-to-be in the object of mind or the process of dissolution in the object of mind or both the process of coming-to-be and the process of dissolution. Or he is mindful of the fact, 'There is an object of mind here,' until understanding and full awareness come about. He remains established in the observation, free, not caught up in any worldly consideration. That is how to practice observation of the objects of mind in the objects of mind with regard to the six sense organs and the six sense objects, O bhikkhus.

"Further, bhikkhus, the practitioner remains established in the observation of the objects of mind in the objects of mind with regard to the Seven Factors of Awakening.

"How does he remain established in the practice of observation of the Seven Factors of Awakening?

1. "When the factor of awakening, mindfulness, is present in him, he is aware, 'Mindfulness is present in me.' When mindfulness is not present in him, he is aware, 'Mindfulness is not present in me.' He is aware when not-yet-born mindfulness is being born and when already-born mindfulness is perfectly developed.
2. "When the factor of awakening, investigation-of-phenomena, is present in him, he is aware, 'Investigation-of-phenomena is present in me.' When investigation-of-phenomena is not present in him, he is aware, 'Investigation-of-phenomena is not present in me.' He is aware when not-yet-born investigation-of-phenomena is being born and when already-born investigation-of-phenomena is perfectly developed.
3. "When the factor of awakening, energy, is present in him, he is aware, 'Energy is present in me.' When energy is not present in him, he is aware, 'Energy is not present in me.' He is aware when not-yet-born energy is being born and when already-born energy is perfectly developed.
4. "When the factor of awakening, joy, is present in him, he is aware, 'Joy is present

in me.' When joy is not present in him, he is aware, 'Joy is not present in me.' He is aware when not-yet-born joy is being born and when already-born joy is perfectly developed.

5. "When the factor of awakening, ease, is present in him, he is aware, 'Ease is present in me.' When ease is not present in him, he is aware, 'Ease is not present in me.' He is aware when not-yet-born ease is being born and when already-born ease is perfectly developed.

6. "When the factor of awakening, concentration, is present in him, he is aware, 'Concentration is present in me.' When concentration is not present in him, he is aware, 'Concentration is not present in me.' He is aware when not-yet-born concentration is being born and when already-born concentration is perfectly developed.

7. "When the factor of awakening, letting go, is present in him, he is aware, 'Letting go is present in me.' When letting go is not present in him, he is aware, 'Letting go is not present in me.' He is aware when not-yet-born letting go is being born and when already-born letting-go is perfectly developed.

"This is how the practitioner remains established in the observation of the objects of mind in the objects of mind with regard to the Seven Factors of Awakening, observation of the objects of mind from within or from without, or observation of the objects of mind from both within and without. He remains established in the observation of the process of coming-to-be in the object of mind or the process of dissolution in the object of mind or both the process of coming-to-be and the process of dissolution. Or he is mindful of the fact, 'There is an object of mind here,' until understanding and full awareness come about. He remains established in the observation, free, not caught up in any worldly consideration. That is how to practice observation of the objects of mind in the objects of mind with regard to the Seven Factors of Awakening, O bhikkhus.

"Further, bhikkhus, a practitioner remains established in the observation of objects of mind in the objects of mind with regard to the Four Noble Truths.

"How, bhikkhus, does the practitioner remain established in the observation of the Four Noble Truths?

"A practitioner is aware 'This is suffering,' as it arises. He is aware, 'This is the cause of the suffering,' as it arises. He is aware, 'This is the end of suffering,' as it arises. He is aware, 'This is the path which leads to the end of suffering,' as it arises.

"This is how the practitioner remains established in the observation of the objects of mind in the objects of mind with regard to the Four Noble Truths, observation of the objects of mind from within or from without, or observation of the objects of mind from both within and without. He remains established in the observation of the process of coming-to-be in the objects of mind or the process of dissolution in the objects of mind or both the process of coming-to-be and the process of dissolution. Or he is mindful of the fact, 'There is an object of mind here,' until understanding and full awareness come about. He remains established in the observation, free, not caught up in any worldly consideration. That is how to practice observation of the objects of mind in the objects of mind with regard to the Four Noble Truths, O bhikkhus."

VI.

"Bhikkhus, he who practices in the Four Establishments of Mindfulness for seven years can expect one of two fruits—the highest understanding in this very life or, if there remains some residue of affliction, he can attain the fruit of no-return.

"Let alone seven years, bhikkhus, whoever practices in the Four Establishments of Mindfulness for six, five, four, three, two years or one year can also expect one of two fruits—either the highest understanding in this very life or, if there remains some residue of affliction, he can attain the fruit of no-return.

"Let alone one year, bhikkhus, whoever practices in the Four Establishments of Mindfulness for seven, six, five, four, three, or two months, one month or half a month can also expect one of two fruits—either the highest understanding in this very life or, if there remains some residue of affliction, he can attain the fruit of no-return.

"Let alone half a month, bhikkhus, whoever practices the Four Establishments of Mindfulness for one week can also expect one of two fruits—either the highest understanding in this very life or, if there remains some residue of affliction, he can attain the fruit of no-return.

"That is why we said that this path, the path of the four grounds for the establishment of mindfulness, is the most wonderful path, which helps beings realize purification, transcend grief and sorrow, destroy pain and anxiety, travel the right path, and realize nirvana."

The bhikkhus were delighted to hear the teaching of the Buddha. They took it to heart and began to put it into practice.

Summary of the Sutra

The Sutra on the Four Establishments of Mindfulness uses the term *ekayana,* which means "one path" in Pali, to signify "the one way to practice." Ekayana is translated in this version of the sutra as "a most wonderful way to help living beings." This term, used by the Buddha to describe the method of the Four Establishments of Mindfulness, gives us an idea of the great importance this practice held in the Buddha's teachings during his lifetime. These teachings have since spread throughout the world, and the foundation of these teachings remains the practice of mindful observation. The Sutra on the Four Establishments of Mindfulness has been studied, practiced, and handed down with special care from generation to generation for over 2,500 years.

The four methods of mindfulness described in the sutra are: (1) mindfulness of the body, (2) mindfulness of the feelings, (3) mindfulness of the mind, and (4) mindfulness of the objects of mind. In the establishment known as the body, the practitioner is fully aware of the breath, the positions of the body, the actions of the body, the various parts of the body, the four elements which comprise the body, and the decomposition of the body as a corpse. In the establishment known as the feelings, the practitioner is fully aware of pleasant, painful, and neutral feelings as they arise, endure, and disappear. He is aware of feelings that have a psychological basis and feelings that have a physiological basis. In the establishment known as the mind, the practitioner is fully aware of states of mind such as desire, hatred, confusion, concentration, dispersion, internal formations, and liberation. In the establishment known as the objects of mind, the practitioner is fully aware of the Five Aggregates that comprise a person (form, feelings, perceptions, mental formations, and consciousness), the sense organs and their objects, the factors that can obstruct understanding and liberation, the factors that can lead to awakening, and the Four Noble Truths concerning suffering and the release from suffering.

As you see, the sutra is divided into six sections: Section One describes the circumstances under which the sutra was delivered and the importance of the teachings of the sutra, and it lists the Four Establishments of Mindfulness. Section Two describes the method of mindfulness of the body in the body. Section Three describes the method of mindfulness of the feelings in the feelings. Section Four describes the method of mindfulness of the mind in the mind. Section Five describes the method of mindfulness of the objects of mind in the objects of mind. Section Six describes the fruits of the practice and the length of time needed in order to realize those fruits.

Mindfulness Exercises

EXERCISES FOR OBSERVING THE BODY

The First Establishment of Mindfulness is the body, which includes the breath, the positions of the body, the actions of the body, the parts of the body, the four elements of which the body is composed, and the dissolution of the body.

Exercise 1: Conscious Breathing

> *He goes to the forest, to the foot of a tree, or to an empty room, sits down cross-legged in the lotus position, holds his body straight, and establishes mindfulness in front of him. He breathes in, aware that he is breathing in. He breathes out, aware that he is breathing out.*

The first practice is the full awareness of breathing. When we breathe in, we know that we are breathing in. When we breathe out, we know that we are breathing out. Practicing in this way, our breathing becomes conscious breathing. This exercise is simple, yet its effects are profound. To succeed, we must put our whole mind into our breathing and nowhere else. As we follow our in-breath, for example, we need to be watchful of distracting thoughts. As soon as a thought such as, "I forgot to turn off the light in the kitchen," arises, our breathing is no longer conscious breathing as we are thinking about something else. To succeed, our mind needs to stay focused on our breathing for the entire length of each breath. As we breathe, our mind is one with our breath, and we become one with our breath. That is the meaning of "mindfulness of the body in the body."

Anyone can succeed in the practice of a single conscious breath. If we continue to breathe consciously for ten breaths, without our mind going astray, then we have taken a valuable step on the path of practice. If we can practice conscious breathing for ten minutes, an important change will take place in us. How can a practice as simple as this bring about such important results and what are the results that it can bring about?

The first result of conscious breathing is returning to ourselves. In everyday life, we often get lost in forgetfulness. Our mind chases after thousands of things, and we rarely take the time to come back to ourselves. When we have been lost in forgetfulness like that for a long time, we lose touch with ourselves, and we feel alienated from ourselves. This phenomenon is very common in our times. Conscious breathing is a marvelous way to return to ourselves. When we are aware of our breath, we come back to ourselves as quick as a flash of lightning. Like a child who returns home after a long journey, we feel the warmth of our hearth, and we find ourselves again. Coming back to ourselves is already a remarkable success on the path of the practice.

The second result of conscious breathing is that we come in contact with life in the present moment, the only moment when we can touch life. The life in us and around us is wonderful and abundant. If we're not free, we can't be in contact with it, and we're not really living our lives. We shouldn't be imprisoned by regrets about the past, anxieties for the future, or attachment and aversion in the present.

To breathe with full awareness is a miraculous way to untie the knots of regret and anxiety and to be in touch with life in the present moment. When we follow our breathing, we are already at ease, no longer dominated by our anxieties and longings. As we breathe consciously, our breath becomes more regular, and peace and joy arise and become more stable with every moment. Relying on our breathing, we come back to ourselves and are able to restore the oneness of our body and mind. This integration allows us to be in real contact with what is happening in the present moment, which is the essence of life.

Exercise 2: Following the Breath

When he breathes in a long breath, he knows, 'I am breathing in a long breath.' When he breathes out a long breath, he knows, 'I am breathing out a long breath.' When he breathes in a short breath, he knows, 'I am breathing in a short breath.' When he breathes out a short breath, he knows, 'I am breathing out a short breath.'

The practitioner follows his breathing very closely and becomes one with his breathing for the entire length of the breath, not allowing any stray thought or idea to enter. This method is called "following the breath." While the mind is following the breath, the mind is the breath and only the breath. In the process of the practice, our breathing naturally becomes more regular, harmonious, and calm, and our mind also becomes more regular, harmonious, and calm. This brings about feelings of joy, peace, and ease in the body. When the mind and the breathing become one, it is only a small step for the body and mind to become one also.

Exercise 3: Oneness of Body and Mind

Breathing in, I am aware of my whole body. Breathing out, I am aware of my whole body.

The third exercise is to bring body and mind into harmony. The element used to bring this about is the breath. In meditation practice, the distinction between body and mind dissolves, and we talk of the oneness of body and mind. In this exercise, the object of our mindfulness is no longer simply the breath, but the whole body itself, as it is unified with the breath.

Some practitioners and commentators, because they attach so much importance to the realization of the states of concentration (Pali: *jhana;* Sanskrit: *dhyana*) of the Four Form Jhanas and the Four Formless Jhanas, have explained the term "whole body" to mean the "whole breath body" and not the physical body of the practitioner. The Patisambhida Magga, Vimutti Magga, and Visuddhi Magga, all well-known commentaries, tell us to concentrate on the tip of our nose, the place where the air enters and goes out from the body, as we breathe. We are not told to follow our breath into our body, because the commentators fear that our body may be too large an object for us to concentrate on. This kind of reasoning has led the commentators to interpret the word "body" (*kaya*) in the sutra as "breath body." But as we read the sutra, we see that the practice of being mindful of the whole "breath body" was already dealt with in the second exercise: "Breathing in a long breath, he knows, 'I am breathing in a long breath.' Breathing out a short breath, he knows, 'I am breathing out a short breath.'" Why then do we need to repeat this exercise?

The first four exercises of the Sutra on the Full Awareness of Breathing (Anapanasati) teach us to focus our attention on the body, so it is natural for the third exercise in the Sutra on the Four Establishments of Mindfulness (Satipatthana) also to focus on the full awareness of the physical body. Nowhere in either sutra are we taught to concentrate on the breath at the tip of the nose. Nowhere are we taught that we shouldn't concentrate on the whole physical body.

In recent times, the Burmese meditation master Mahasi Sayadaw taught the method of being attentive to the inflation and contraction of the abdomen caused by the in-breath and the out-breath. Using this method, the practitioner can realize concentration easily, but it isn't described by the Mahasi as a method of awareness of breathing. The basic reason for doing this practice, according to the Mahasi, is that understanding (*prajña*) arises naturally when there is concentration. Perhaps the reason Mahasi Sayadaw doesn't describe this method as a practice of awareness of breathing is because of traditional prejudice that conscious breathing should not follow the breath into the body and down into the abdomen.

Here it may be useful to say something about the purpose of concentration. Right Concentration (*samyak samadhi*), one stage of the Noble Eightfold Path, leads to an awareness and deep observation of the object of concentration and eventually to awakened understanding. The Pali compound word *samatha-vipassana* (Sanskrit: *samatha-vipashyana*) means "stopping-observing," "calming-illuminating," or "concentrating-understanding."

There are also states of concentration that encourage the practitioner to escape from the complexities of suffering and existence, rather than face them directly in order to transform them. These can be called "wrong concentration." The Four Form Jhanas and the Four Formless Jhanas are states of meditational concentration which the Buddha practiced with teachers such as Alara Kalama and Uddaka Ramaputta, and he rejected them as not leading to liberation from suffering. These states of concentration probably found their way back into the sutras around two hundred years after the Buddha passed into *mahapari-nirvana*. The results of these concentrations are to hide reality from the practitioner, so we can assume that they shouldn't be considered Right Concentration. To dwell in these concentrations for a duration of time for the sake of healing may be one thing, but to escape in them for a long time isn't what the Buddha recommended.

In the third exercise, the practitioner uses her breathing to bring body and mind together as one, so the object of concentration is simultaneously body, mind, and breath. This condition, known as "oneness of body and mind," is one of total integration. In our daily lives, we often find our mind and our body separated. Our body may be here, while our mind is somewhere else, perhaps lost in the distant past or floating in a distant future. Through mindfulness, we can realize the oneness of body and mind, and we're able to restore the wholeness of ourselves. In this condition, every practice will take us back to the source, which is the oneness of body and mind, and we open to a real encounter with life.

When body and mind are one, the wounds in our hearts, minds, and bodies begin to heal. As long as there is separation between body and mind, these wounds can't heal. During sitting meditation, the three elements of breath, body, and mind are calmed, and gradually they become one. When peace is established in one of the three elements, the other two will soon have peace also. For example, if the body is in a very stable position and all the muscles and the nervous system are relaxed, then the mind and breath are immediately influenced, and they too gradually become calmed. Similarly, if we practice conscious breathing in the right way, our breathing becomes more regular, calm, and harmonious with every moment, and this regularity, calmness, and harmony of the breathing will spread to our body and mind, and the body and mind will benefit from it. It's only by these kinds of processes that the oneness of body and mind will be achieved. When there's oneness of body and mind, the breathing serves as "harmonizer," and we realize peace, joy, and ease, the first fruits of meditation practice.

Exercise 4: Calming

Breathing in, I calm my body. Breathing out, I calm my body.

This exercise, a continuation of the third, uses the breath to realize peace and calm in our whole body. When our body is not at peace, it's hard for our mind to be at peace. Therefore, we should use our breathing to help the functions of our body be smooth and peaceful. If we're gasping for breath or if our breath is irregular, we can't calm the functions of our body. So the first thing is to harmonize our breathing. Our in-breaths and out-breaths should flow smoothly and lightly. When our breath is harmonious, our body is also. Our breath needs to be light and even and not audible. It should flow smoothly, like a small stream of water running down fine sand into the ocean. The more subtle our breath is, the more peaceful our body and mind will be. When we breathe in, we can feel the breath entering our body and calming all the cells of our body. When we breathe out, we feel the exhalation taking with it all our tiredness, irritation, and anxiety.

As we breathe, we can recite the following *gatha* to ourselves:
Breathing in, I calm my body.
Breathing out, I smile.
Dwelling in the present moment,
I know this is a wonderful moment.

We know that when we're meditating, body and mind are one, so we only need to calm our body in order to calm our mind. When we smile, we demonstrate the peace and joy of body and mind. Feelings of peace and joy are the nourishment of the practitioner and help the practitioner go far on the path of practice. To learn more about this, you are encouraged to practice the fifth and sixth exercises of the Sutra on the Full Awareness of Breathing. These two exercises are designed to help the practitioner nourish herself with the joy of meditational concentration. The essence of meditation practice is to come back to dwell in the present moment and to observe what is happening in the present moment. "A wonderful moment" means that the practitioner can see the wonders of life in her body, mind, and breathing and can make the feelings of peace and happiness stable and strong.

Although we are now discussing the part of the sutra that teaches full awareness of the body in the body, since there are very close links between the body and the feelings, we should not hesitate to cross freely the boundary between the establishment of the body and the establishment of the feelings. As we already know, the peace of the body is the peace of the mind.

In exercises three and four, the practitioner follows the breath while returning to be one with the body and calming the whole of the body. Obviously, while practicing these breathing exercises, all your organs of sense perception—eyes, ears, nose, and tongue—are closed off so that the images of the world around don't come in and agitate the peace within. To return to the body in this way is also to return to the mind.

From time to time, we feel tired, and everything we do or say seems to come out wrong and create misunderstanding. We may think, "Today is not my day." At times like this, it's best simply to return to our body, cut off all contact, and close the doors of the senses. Following our breathing, we can collect our mind, body, and breath, and they will become one. We will have a feeling of warmth, like someone sitting inside by a fireplace while the wind and rain are raging outside. This method can be practiced anywhere at any time, not just in the meditation hall. We come back in contact with ourselves and make ourselves whole again.

We shouldn't think that to close the doors of the sense perceptions is to close ourselves off from life and the world, to sever our contact with life. When we're not truly ourselves, when we're divided and dispersed, we're not really in contact with life. The contact is profound only when we are really ourselves. If we're not ourselves in the present moment, when we look at the blue sky, we don't really see the blue sky. When we hold the hand of a child, we aren't really holding the hand of a child. When we drink tea, we're not really drinking tea.

Therefore, the wholeness of ourselves is the basis of any meaningful contact. We can realize the wholeness of ourselves by means of conscious breathing, which brings us back to our body and mind. Realizing the wholeness of ourselves is also to renew ourselves in every moment. We become fresh, and others enjoy being with us. When we renew ourselves, we see everything else as new. The Bamboo Forest Zen Master once said: "Everything I touch becomes new."

Exercise 5: Positions of the Body

Moreover, when a practitioner walks, he is aware, 'I am walking.' When he is standing, he is aware, 'I am standing.' When he is sitting, he is aware, 'I am sitting.' When he is lying down, he is aware, 'I am lying down.' In whatever position his body happens to be, he is aware of the position of his body.

This exercise is the observation in mindfulness of the positions of the body. This is not just an exercise to be practiced at the time of sitting meditation or in the meditation hall. The meditation practices taught in the Sutra on the Four Establishments of Mindfulness can be used all the day long to help the practitioner remain in mindfulness. When doing walking meditation in the meditation hall or outside, the practitioner can combine her breathing with her steps in order to remain steadily established in mindfulness. Before beginning any kind of walking meditation, we can recite the following gatha:

> The mind can go in a thousand directions,
> But on this beautiful path, I walk in peace.
> With each step, a gentle wind blows.
> With each step, a flower blooms.

Anytime we sit down, we can follow our breath and use this gatha:

> Sitting here
> is like sitting under the Bodhi tree.
> My body is mindfulness itself,
> entirely free from distraction.

We can use our breathing in order to be aware of the positions of sitting and standing. When we're standing in a line waiting to buy a ticket, or when we're just sitting down and waiting for anything, we can recite the gatha, "Breathing in, I calm my body," in order to continue dwelling in mindfulness and to calm our body and mind.

Exercise 6: Bodily Actions

> *Moreover, when the practitioner is going forward or backward, he applies full awareness to his going forward or backward. When he looks in front or looks behind, bends down or stands up, he also applies full awareness to what he is doing. He applies full awareness to*

wearing the sanghati robe or carrying the alms bowl. When he eats or drinks, chews or savors the food, he applies full awareness to all this. When passing excrement or urinating, he applies full awareness to this. When he walks, stands, lies down, sits, sleeps or wakes up, speaks or is silent, he shines his awareness on all this.

This exercise is the observation and awareness of the actions of the body. This is the fundamental practice of the monk. When I was first ordained as a novice over sixty years ago, the first book my master gave me to learn by heart was a book of short verses (gathas) to be practiced while washing your hands, brushing your teeth, washing your face, putting on your clothes, sweeping the courtyard, relieving yourself, having a bath, and so on. On hearing the sound of the bell, we would breathe consciously and recite this gatha:

> Hearing the sound of the bell,
> the afflictions are lifted.
> Understanding grows strong,
> and the awakened mind is born.

Practicing breathing in combination with reciting a gatha helps us dwell more easily in mindfulness. Mindfulness makes every action of our body more serene, and we become master of our body and mind. Mindfulness nurtures the power of concentration in us. Many of the gathas in the book I was given, *Gathas for Everyday Use*, a text by Chinese master Du Ti, were taken from the Avatamsaka Sutra. I have written a book of gathas in the same spirit, *Present Moment, Wonderful Moment*.[2] These gathas are very easy to use and can also be combined with conscious breathing.

Without mindfulness, our actions are often hurried and abrupt. As we practice the sixth exercise, we may find that our actions slow down. If a novice applies himself to the practice of the sixth exercise, he'll see that his everyday actions become harmonious, graceful, and measured. Mindfulness becomes visible in his actions and speech. When any action is placed in the light of mindfulness, the body and mind become relaxed, peaceful, and joyful. The sixth exercise is one to be used day and night throughout our entire life.

Exercise 7: Parts of the Body

> *Further, the practitioner meditates on his very own body from the soles of the feet upwards and then from the hair on top of the head downwards, a body contained inside the skin and full of all the impurities which belong to the body: 'Here is the hair of the head, the*

---

[2] Thich Nhat Hanh, Present Moment, Wonderful Moment (Berkeley, CA: Parallax Press, 1990).

hairs on the body, the nails, teeth, skin, flesh, sinews, bones, bone marrow, kidneys, heart, liver, diaphragm, spleen, lungs, intestines, bowels, excrement, bile, phlegm, pus, blood, sweat, fat, tears, grease, saliva, mucus, synovic fluid, urine.'

This exercise brings us into even deeper contact with our body. Here we observe the body in all its parts, from the hair on the head to the skin on the soles of the feet. In the process of our observation, we scan all the parts of the body, including the brain, heart, lungs, gall bladder, spleen, blood, urine, and so forth. The Buddha gives us the example of a farmer pouring the contents of a sack filled with a variety of seeds onto the floor and then observing and identifying each kind of seed: "This is rice, these are beans, these are sesame seeds."

We use our conscious breathing in order to observe mindfully all the parts of the body. For example: "Breathing in, I am aware of the hair on my head. Breathing out, I know that this is the hair on my head." Breathing consciously helps us dwell in mindfulness more easily and sustain the work of observing each part of the body. In addition to the conscious breathing, we can use the method of silently calling each part of the body by name to enable these parts to become increasingly clear in the light of mindfulness.

Why do we need to observe in mindfulness the different parts of the body? First of all, it is to be in contact with the body. We often have the impression that we're already totally in touch with our body, but often we're wrong. Between us and our body there can be a large separation, and our body remains a stranger to us. Sometimes we hate our body. There are even people who see their body as a prison and a place of punishment. To come back to our body is to become familiar with it and to establish harmony with it. We know that if our body isn't happy, we're not happy, and so we want our body to be calm and peaceful. To do so, we come back to our body and make peace with it.

We can try touching the different parts of our body to make their acquaintance. We should touch each part in an affectionate and caring way. For several decades, our eyes, feet, and heart have done their work devotedly and faithfully with us and for us, but we never really give them much attention or express our gratitude to them. It's necessary to establish a close relationship with our body.

The second reason for mindfully observing the different parts of the body is that each part can be the door to liberation and awakening. At first we'll only recognize the presence of the part of the body being observed, but later we'll come to see its true nature. Every hair on our head and every cell in our body contains the entire universe. Observing the interdependent nature of a single hair can help us to see into the nature of the universe.

The exercise of observing every part of the body begins with the hair on the head and goes down to the skin on the soles of the feet. Sometimes we observe just one part of the body deeply, such as our eyes, heart, or toe. In the process of observation from the head to the feet, some observations may spring up in our mind. For example, as we pass our heart, we may think, "My friend John has a heart condition. I must visit him soon to see if he's all right." We can note these observations and then continue with the work of observing the remaining parts of the body. Later we can return to those observations.

Exercise 8: Body and Universe

Further, in whichever position his body happens to be, the practitioner passes in review the elements which constitute the body: 'In this body is the earth element, the water element, the fire element, and the air element.'

This exercise shows us the interrelationship of our body and all that is in the universe. It's one of the principal ways of witnessing for ourselves the nonself, unborn, and never-dying nature of all that is. Seeing things in this way can liberate and awaken us.

The sutra teaches us that we should be aware of the presence of earth, water, fire, and air elements in our body. These are the Four Great Elements (Sanskrit: *mahabhuta*), also referred to as the realms (Sanskrit: *dhatu*). The earth element represents the hard, solid nature of matter. The water element represents the liquid, permeating nature. The fire element represents heat, and the air element represents movement. The Dhatuvibhanga Sutra and the second version of the sutra on mindfulness in this book both refer to six elements—the two additional elements are space (Sanskrit: *akasa*) and consciousness (Sanskrit: *vijñana*).

Our bodies are more than three-fourths water. When the practitioner looks deeply in order to see the water in his body, not only does he see the liquid, permeating nature of the blood, sweat, saliva, tears, and urine, but he also sees the water element in every cell of his body. There are clouds in the body, because without clouds there can be no rain, and we won't have any water to drink or grains and vegetables to eat. We see earth in us, earth as the minerals in our body. We also see that earth is alive in us because, thanks to Mother Earth, we have food to eat. We see air in us, air representing movement. Without air we could not survive, since we, as every other species on Earth, need air to live.

The practitioner observes her body mindfully to see all that is in it and to see the interrelated nature of herself and the universe. She sees that his life is not just present in her own body, and she transcends the erroneous view that she's just her body. In the book *The Sun My Heart*, I refer to the sun as our second heart, a heart which lies outside our body but which is as essential for our body as the heart inside our body.[3] When the heart inside the body ceases to function, we know very well that we will die, but we often forget that if the heart outside our body, the sun, ceases to function, we will also die immediately. When we observe mindfully the interdependent nature of our body, we see our life outside our body, and we transcend the boundary between self and nonself. This practice of mindful observation helps us go beyond such limiting concepts as birth and death.

Exercise 9: Body As Impermanent

The Nine Contemplations (the nine stages of decomposition of a corpse):
1. *The corpse is bloated, blue, and festering.*
2. *The corpse is crawling with insects and worms. Crows, hawks, vultures, and wolves are tearing it apart to eat.*
3. *All that is left is a skeleton with some flesh and blood still clinging to it.*
4. *All that is left is a skeleton with some blood stains, but no more flesh.*
5. *All that is left is a skeleton with no more blood stains.*

---

[3] Thich Nhat Hanh, The Sun My Heart (Berkeley, CA: Parallax Press, 1988).

6. *All that is left is a collection of scattered bones—here an arm, here a shin, here a skull, and so forth.*
7. *All that is left is a collection of bleached bones.*
8. *All that is left is a collection of dried bones.*
9. *The bones have decomposed, and only a pile of dust is left.*

This exercise helps us see the impermanent and decomposing nature of our body. The objects of our mindful observation are the nine stages of the decomposition of a corpse. When we first read this, we may feel that this is not a pleasant meditation. But the effect of this practice can be very great. It can be liberating and can bring us much peace and joy. The practitioner observes mindfully in order to see the corpse at each of these stages and to see that it is inevitable that her own body will pass through the same stages.

In former times, practitioners would actually sit in cemeteries and observe corpses in these various stages of decomposition. Of course, today, decomposing bodies aren't exposed for us to view. But we can visualize them according to the description in the sutra. This exercise should be practiced by those who are in good mental and physical health. It shouldn't be practiced by those who have not yet mastered desire and aversion. Its intention is not to make us weary of life, but to help us see how precious life is; not to make us pessimistic, but to help us see the impermanent nature of life so that we don't waste our lives. If we have the courage to see things as they are, our meditation will have beneficial results. When we see the impermanent nature of things, we appreciate their true value.

Have you ever stayed up at night to see a Cereus cactus flower open? The flower opens and dies in a few hours, but because we're aware of that, we appreciate its wondrous fragrance and beauty. We can be in real contact with the flower and not be sad or depressed when it fades, because we knew before it opened how ephemeral its life was.

Our dear ones who live with us and the beautiful and precious beings around us are all wonderful cactus flowers. If we can see their true nature as well as their outward form, we will know how to value their presence in the present moment. If we know how to value them, we'll have the time to be in real contact with them, and we'll take care of them, make them happy, and therefore be happier ourselves.

These Nine Contemplations help us see the preciousness of life. They teach us how to live lightly and freshly, without being caught by attachments and aversions.

REMARKS ON THE FIRST NINE EXERCISES

When we practice the above nine exercises offered by the Buddha for observing the body in the body, we concentrate either on the breath, the body, the positions of the body, the actions of the body, the different parts of the body, the elements which form the body, or the decomposition of the body. When we observe the body this way, we are in direct contact with it, and we are able to see the process of coming-to-be and ceasing-to-be in the constituents that comprise the body. In the first version of the sutra, at the end of each meditation exercise to observe the body in the body, we read:

> This is how the practitioner remains established in the observation of the body in the body, observation of the body from within or from without, or observation of the body from both within and without. He remains established in the observation of the process of coming-to-be in the body or the process of dissolution in the body or both the process of coming-to-be and the process of dissolution. Or he is mindful of the fact, 'There is a body here,' until understanding and full awareness come about. He remains established in the observation, free, not caught up in any worldly consideration.

We should remember that the breathing, the positions of the body, the movements of the body, and the parts of the body all belong to the body and are the body. To be in touch with these aspects and to be able to see the process of birth and death and the nonself and interdependent nature of the body is the meaning of mindful observation of the body.

Therefore, the teachings of impermanence, selflessness, and interdependent origination—the three basic observations of Buddhism—are realized directly through the practice of the nine exercises for mindfully observing the body. These nine exercises can liberate and awaken us to the way things are.

In the second version of the sutra, the description of each body meditation exercise is as follows:

> This is how the practitioner is aware of body as body, both within and without, and establishes mindfulness in the body with understanding, insight, clarity, and realization. This is called being aware of body as body.

The words *recognition, insight, clarity,* and *realization* here mean that the practitioner recognizes, sees, sheds light on, and realizes the impermanent and interdependent nature of the body and all that is, by means of the mindful observation of the body.

Observing the impermanent, selfless, and interdependent nature of all that is doesn't lead us to feel aversion for life. On the contrary, it helps us see the preciousness of all that lives. Liberation doesn't mean running away from or destroying life. Many people present Buddhism as a path that denies life, that transcends the world of the Five Aggregates (Sanskrit: *skandha*) of form, feelings, perceptions, mental formations, and consciousness. To present Buddhism in this way is no different from saying that the object of our practice is to arrive at the absence of life or nothingness.

In the Dhammacakka Sutta, the first Dharma talk given by the Buddha in the Deer Park, the Buddha taught that to be attached to existence (Sanskrit: *bhava*) is no worse than to be attached to nonexistence (Sanskrit: *abhava*). In the Kaccayana Gotta Sutta, the Buddha also taught that reality is not to be found in terms of existence or nonexistence. His meaning is perfectly clear: suffering is not brought about by life, the Five Skandhas, or the selfless and interdependent nature of all that is. The cause of ill-being is our ignorance. Because we're not able to see that the true nature of life is impermanence, selflessness, and interdependence, we become attached to things, believing that they're permanent. From this thinking arise the roots of affliction and the internal formations or knots: craving, hatred, pride, doubt, and so forth. Impermanence, selflessness, and interdependence are the essential conditions for life. Without impermanence, how can the corn seed become a corn plant and how can the baby grow up and go to school?

In fact, it's because of impermanence, selflessness, and interdependence that things come into existence, mature, decay, and cease to be. Birth, decay, and ceasing to be are the necessary steps of the lives of all species. Presenting impermanence, selflessness, and interdependence as problematic, we senselessly make life unacceptable. We need to do the opposite; we need to praise them as essential elements of life. Only when we're not able to recognize these attributes as they are do we get caught in the knots of attachment and sorrow.

The Ratnakuta Sutra gives the example of someone who throws a clod of earth at a dog. When the clod hits the dog, he runs after it and barks furiously at it. The dog doesn't know that the thing responsible for his pain isn't the clod of earth but the man who threw it. The sutra teaches:

> In the same way, the ordinary man caught in dualistic conceptions is accustomed to thinking that the Five Aggregates are the root of his suffering, but in fact the root of suffering is the lack of understanding about the impermanent, selfless, and interdependent nature of the Five Aggregates.

Because we don't understand correctly, we become attached to things, and then we're caught by them. In the sutra, the term "aggregate" (Pali:

khanda; Sanskrit: *skandha*) and the term "aggregate of clinging" (Pali: *upadanakkhanda;* Sanskrit: *upadanaskandha*) are used. Skandhas are the five elements that give rise to life, and the upadana skandhas are the five elements as objects of attachment. The root of suffering isn't the skandhas but the attachment that binds us. There are people who, because of their incorrect understanding of what the root of suffering is, instead of dealing with their attitude of attachment, think they have to deal with their organs of sense and the aggregates, and so they fear form, sound, smell, taste, touch, and objects of mind and feel aversion for the body, feelings, perceptions, mental formations, and consciousness.

The Buddha was someone who, because he wasn't attached to things, lived in peace, joy, and freedom with a healthy and fresh vigor. He always had a smile on his lips, and his presence created a fresh atmosphere around him. There are many stories in the sutras which show how much the Buddha loved life and knew how to appreciate the beautiful things around him. On many occasions, he pointed out beautiful scenery to Ananda, such as the sun setting on Vulture Peak, the golden rice fields surrounded by green paths, the fresh green landscape of the Bamboo Forest Monastery, and the lovely town of Vaisali. The Buddha was not afraid of beautiful things, because he was able to see the impermanent nature of everything, beautiful or ugly. He didn't chase after things, and he didn't run away from them either. The way of freedom isn't running away from the Five Aggregates, but coming face to face with them in order to understand their true nature.

If we cut flowers from our garden to place on the altar, that is because we acknowledge the beauty of those flowers. All we can say is, "Although these flowers are beautiful, their beauty is fragile. When, in a few days time, these flowers die, their beauty will die with them." We understand this, and when the flowers wilt in a few days, we won't suffer or feel sad. Because we can see the impermanent nature of the flowers, we can appreciate all the more the beauty of each flower. To observe the impermanence of things is not to reject them, but to be in contact with them with deep understanding, without being caught in desire and attachment.

Freedom in Buddhism is the freedom which comes about by being awake and understanding. A practitioner doesn't need to struggle with desire. The two basic meditation sutras, the Sutra on the Four Establishments of Mindfulness and the Sutra on the Full Awareness of Breathing, both shed light on this principle: "When his mind is desiring something, the practitioner is aware, 'My mind is desiring'" (Satipatthana Sutta), and "Breathing in, I am aware of the functions of my mind" (Anapanasati Sutta). In identifying the mind of desire, in observing the nature of that mind and the nature of the object of desire, we'll see the impermanence, selflessness, and interdependence of it, and we'll no longer be dominated by that state of mind.

For many generations, some Buddhists have presented Buddhism as a path that destroys desire, and they have described liberated persons as emaciated *arhats* with wrinkled skin and no vitality. We should define what is meant by desire. If we've had nothing to eat for three days, we feel like eating. Is that desire? Is the natural desire for the indispensable elements of life a desire we need to destroy? To eat when hungry, to drink when thirsty, is that to go against the path which leads to emancipation? But if so, then Buddhism would be a path that flees from and destroys life.

We know very well that to eat and drink enough are necessary to nourish our body and keep us strong. We also know that eating and drinking excessively can destroy our bodies. So we can say that to eat and drink so that the body is strong and healthy is to walk on the path of emancipation, while to eat and drink in a way that causes our body and others to suffer is to go against the way of liberation. In the first case desire isn't present, in the second case desire is present.

Other Buddhists have opposed the image of the emaciated arhat destroying desire and have described liberated persons as fresh, healthy bodhisattvas, beautiful to look at and full of vigor. The image of the bodhisattva is very close to the image of the Buddha entering life with a heart of love and compassion and a smile on his lips. Although the Buddha enjoyed the solitary life, he never refused to go deeply into the world in order to help living beings.

To know how to appreciate a beautiful sunset is not desire, if we "remain established in the observation, free and not caught up in any worldly consideration" (Satipatthana Sutta). If we are able to see impermanence, selflessness, and interdependence, we are awake. To swim in a cool stream, to drink a glass of clear water, to eat a sweet orange, and to know how to appreciate the coolness, the clarity, and the sweetness, is not desire if we are not attached to these things. In the Southern tradition of Buddhism, and to some extent in the Northern tradition, generations of Buddhists have expressed fear of peace and joy and have not dared to practice peace and joy. The tenth exercise is taken from the second version of the sutra (see Appendix). It is a practice of peace and joy.

Exercise 10: Healing with Joy

Further, bhikkhus, a practitioner is aware of body as body, when, thanks to having put aside the Five Desires, a feeling of bliss arises during his concentration and saturates every part of his body.

Further, bhikkhus, a practitioner who is aware of body as body, feels the joy which arises during concentration saturate every part of his body. There is no part of his body this feeling of joy, born during concentration, does not reach.

Further, bhikkhus, a practitioner who is aware of body as body, experiences a feeling of happiness which arises with the disappearance of the feeling of joy and permeates his whole body. This feeling of happiness which arises with the disappearance of the feeling of joy reaches every part of his body.

Further, bhikkhus, a practitioner who is aware of body as body, envelops the whole of his body with a clear, calm mind, filled with understanding.

The purpose of this exercise is to bring about ease, peace, and joy; to heal the wounds of the body as well as of the heart and mind; to nourish us as we grow in the practice of joy; and to enable us to go far on the path of practice.

When the practitioner is able to put an end to agitation, desire, and hatred, he sits down in the lotus position and concentrates on his breath, and he feels a sense of ease and freedom. As a result, a feeling of joy arises in his body. You can practice according to the following exercises:

1. I am breathing in and making my whole body calm and at peace. I am breathing out

and making my whole body calm and at peace. (Exercise 4 again.)
2. I am breathing in and feeling joyful. I am breathing out and feeling joyful. (This is the fifth exercise of the Anapanasati.)
3. I am breathing in and feeling happy. I am breathing out and feeling happy. (This is the sixth exercise of the Anapanasati.)
4. I am breathing in and making my mind happy and at peace. I am breathing out and making my mind happy and at peace. (This is the tenth exercise of the Anapanasati.)

While practicing in this way, the practitioner feels the elements of joy and peace permeate every cell of his body. Please read the following excerpt from the second version:

> Like the bath attendant, who, after putting powdered soap into a basin, mixes it with water until the soap paste has water in every part of it, so the practitioner feels the bliss that is born when the desires of the sense realms are put aside, saturate every part of his body.

The feeling of joy that's born when the practitioner lets go of his life of agitation, desire, and hatred will strengthen and penetrate more deeply when he has mastered the way of applying his mind:

> Like a spring within a mountain whose clear, pure water flows out and down all

sides of that mountain and bubbles up in places where water has not previously entered, saturating the entire mountain, in the same way joy, born during concentration, permeates the whole of the practitioner's body; it is present everywhere.

When the state of happiness is really present, the joy of the mind settles down to allow happiness to become steadier and deeper. For as long as the joy is still there, there goes with it, to a greater or lesser extent, conceptualization and excitement. "Joy" is a translation of the Sanskrit word *piti*, and "happiness" is a translation of *sukha*. The following example is often used to compare joy with happiness: Someone traveling in the desert who sees a stream of cool water experiences joy. When he drinks the water, he experiences happiness.

Just as the different species of blue, pink, red, and white lotus, which grow up from the bottom of a pond of clear water and appear on the surface of that pond, have their tap roots, subsidiary roots, leaves, and flowers all full of the water of that pond, and there is no part of the plant which does not contain the water, so the feeling of happiness which arises with the disappearance of joy permeates the whole of the practitioner's body, and there is no part which it does not penetrate.

At the time of the meditation, the practitioner feels happy and at peace. He lets his consciousness of this peace and happiness embrace his whole body, so that his body is saturated by it:

> Just as someone who puts on a very long robe which reaches from his head to his feet, and there is no part of his body which is not covered by this robe, so the practitioner with a clear, calm mind envelops his whole body in understanding and leaves no part of the body uncovered. This is how the practitioner is aware of the body as the body, both within and without, and establishes mindfulness in the body with recognition, insight, clarity, and realization. This is called being aware of the body as the body.

As we've already seen, the function of this exercise is to nourish us with joy and happiness and to heal the wounds within us. But we have no doubts about letting go of this joy in order to embark on the work of observation. Joy and happiness come about because of physical and psychological conditions and are as impermanent as all other physical and psychological phenomena. Only when, thanks to mindful observation, we realize the impermanent, selfless, and interdependent nature of all that is, can we achieve freedom and liberation.

EXERCISES FOR OBSERVING THE FEELINGS

Exercise 11: Identifying Feelings

Whenever the practitioner has a pleasant feeling, he is aware, 'I am experiencing a pleasant feeling.' Whenever he has a painful feeling, he is aware, 'I am experiencing a painful feeling.' Whenever he experiences a feeling which is neither pleasant nor painful, he is aware, 'I am experiencing a neutral feeling.'

There are three sorts of feelings: pleasant, unpleasant, and neutral. The teaching of this exercise is to identify and be in touch with these feelings as they arise, endure, and fade away.

When there is an unpleasant feeling, the practitioner is not in a hurry to chase it away. She comes back to her conscious breathing and observes, "Breathing in, I know that an unpleasant feeling has arisen within me. Breathing out, I know that this unpleasant feeling is present in me." Whenever there is a pleasant or a neutral feeling, she practices mindful observation in accordance with that feeling. She knows that her feeling is her, and that for the moment she is that feeling. She is neither drowned in nor terrorized by that feeling, nor does she reject it. This is the most effective way to be in contact with feelings. If we call a pleasant, unpleasant, or neutral feeling by its name, we identify it clearly and recognize it more deeply. Our attitude of not clinging to or rejecting our feelings is the attitude of letting go (Pali: *upekkha,* Sanskrit: *upeksa*) and is an important part of meditation practice. Letting go is one of the Four Unlimited Minds (Sanskrit: *brahmavihara*), which are love, compassion, joy, and letting go.

A person is comprised of the Five Aggregates—form (the body), feelings, perceptions, mental formations, and consciousness. Each aggregate is a river. Our body is a river in which every cell is a drop of water, and all of them are in constant transformation and movement. There is also a river of feelings in us, in which every feeling is a drop of water. Each of these feelings—pleasant, unpleasant, neutral—relies on all other feelings to be born, mature, and disappear. To observe the feelings is to sit on the bank of the river of feelings and identify each feeling as it is arises, matures, and disappears.

Our feelings usually play an important part in directing our thoughts and our mind. Our thoughts arise and become linked to each other around the feelings that are present. When we are mindful of our feeling, the situation begins to change. The feeling is no longer the only thing present in us, and it is transformed under the light of our awareness. Therefore, it no longer sweeps us along the way it did before there was mindfulness of the feeling. If we continue to observe the feeling mindfully, we will be able to see its substance and its roots. This empowers the observer. When we are able to see the nature of something, we are able to transcend it and not be led astray or corrupted by it anymore.

Exercise 12: Seeing the Roots of Feelings and Identifying Neutral Feelings

When he experiences a pleasant feeling based in the body, he is aware, 'I am experiencing a pleasant feeling based in the body.' When he experiences a pleasant feeling based in the mind, he is aware, 'I am experiencing a pleasant feeling based in the mind.' When he experiences a painful feeling based in the body, he is aware, 'I am experiencing a painful feeling based in the body.' When he experiences a painful feeling based in the mind, he is aware, 'I am experiencing a painful feeling based in the mind.' When he experiences a neutral feeling based in the body, he is aware, 'I am experiencing a neutral feeling based in the body.' When he experiences a neutral feeling based in the mind, he is aware, 'I am experiencing a neutral feeling based in the mind.'

This exercise is a continuation of Exercise 11 and has the capacity to help us see the roots and the substance of the feelings we have. Our feelings—pleasant, unpleasant, and neutral—can have a physical, physiological, or psychological root. When we mindfully observe our feelings, we discover their roots. For example, if you have an unpleasant feeling because you stayed up late the night before, your unpleasant feeling has a physiological root. Nevertheless, to be able to identify the roots of your feelings is not enough. We have to look more deeply in order to see how these feelings manifest and to understand their true substance. To know a feeling is not just to see its roots but also to see its flowering and its fruits.

When some people take a sip of whiskey or inhale from a cigarette, for example, they may have a pleasant feeling. If they observe this feeling mindfully, they can see its physiological and psychological roots. We know that not everyone shares the same pleasant feeling when they drink whiskey or smoke cigarettes. If some other people were to do either of these two things, they may cough or choke, and the feeling would be unpleasant. Thus the roots of that feeling are not as simple as they might appear at first. The elements of habit, time, and our own psychology and physiology are all present in the roots of any feeling. Looking into our feeling, we can see physiological, physical, and psychological habits; not only our own habits, but also those of the society whose products we are consuming.

Looking into our feeling, we see the nature of whiskey and the nature of tobacco. Looking into the glass of whiskey, we can see the grains that are needed for its production. We can see the effect that the alcohol will have on our body now and in the near future. We can see the connection between the consumption of alcohol and car accidents. We can see the link between the consumption of alcohol and the severe lack of food in the world. We have squandered a large amount of grains in producing alcohol and meat, while in many places in the world, children and adults are dying for want of grain to eat. An economist at the University of Paris once said: "If the western world were to consume fifty percent less alcohol and meat, the problem of starvation in the world could be solved." If we look into any one thing with the eyes of mindful observation, we can see the roots and the results of it. If we mindfully observe a feeling, we can see the roots of that feeling and the results it is likely to produce. The mindful observation of a feeling can lead to a deep insight into the nature of life.

When we hear someone praise us, we may have a pleasant feeling. That pleasant feeling also needs to be examined. Obviously we have the right to accept a pleasant feeling, but we know that in our meditation practice we need to observe mindfully in order to have clear insight into the nature of our feeling. If in our mindful observation, we see that those words of praise were based in flattery rather than reality, then we discover that our pleasant feeling arose out of ignorance and self-love. Such a pleasant feeling can take us farther along the path of illusion. When we see that, the pleasant feeling disappears, and we come back to the ground of reality with both feet planted firmly. The danger of being deluded no longer exists, and we become healthy again. The pleasant feeling we have when we drink alcohol will also disappear when we see its roots and its effects. When pleasant feelings like this disappear, they can give rise to pleasant feelings of another kind, such as the awareness that we are now living in a way that leads to health and awakened understanding. Pleasant feelings of the second kind are healthy because they nourish us and others and cause no harm.

Even though we feel that the words of praise are in harmony with the truth, we should continue to observe the pleasant feeling brought about by those words of praise. The work of mindful observation helps us avoid pride or arrogance—the two things which above all obstruct our progress on the path. We see that if we keep on with what we have started, we will make additional progress, and the words of praise, instead of making us proud or arrogant, become elements of encouragement for us. If we observe mindfully like that, the pleasant feeling on hearing words of praise becomes a healthy feeling and has a nourishing effect.

When we observe our feelings, we can see their relative nature. It is our way of seeing the world that determines the nature of our feelings. One person while working might feel that work is nothing but agony, and he will only feel happy when he is not working. There are other people, however, who feel uneasy when they have nothing to do and would be happy with any work rather than doing nothing. In the latter case, work brings joy, a pleasant feeling, while in the former case, work gives rise to unpleasant feelings, such as boredom or drudgery. Often we do not see that we have all the conditions necessary for happiness, and we go looking for happiness in another place or in the future. To be able to breathe can be a great source of real happiness, but often, unless we have a congested nose or asthma, we are not able to realize that. To be able to see beautiful colors and forms is happiness, but often only after we have lost our sight do we become aware of this. Having sound and healthy limbs to be able to run and jump, living in an atmosphere of freedom, not being separated from our family—all these things and thousands more can be elements of happiness. But we rarely remember, and happiness slips from our grasp as we chase other things which we believe to be necessary for our happiness. Generally, only after we lose an element of happiness do we appreciate it. Awareness of these precious elements of happiness is itself the practice of Right Mindfulness. We can use conscious breathing to shine light on their presence:

Breathing in,
I know that I have two good eyes.
Breathing out,
I know that I have two able hands.
Breathing in,
I know that I am holding my child in my arms.
Breathing out,
I know that I am sitting with my family at the table.

Exercises such as these nourish Right Mindfulness and bring much happiness into our daily lives.

Peace, joy, and happiness are above all the awareness that we have the conditions for happiness. Thus mindfulness is the basic and essential ingredient for happiness. If you do not know that you are happy, it means that you are not happy. Most of us only remember that not having a toothache is happiness at the time when we have a toothache. We are not aware of the joy of our non-toothache, because we do not practice mindfulness.

When a feeling is born in us, we know that it is born. As long as that feeling continues to be present, we know that it continues to be present. We look into it mindfully in order to be able to recognize its nature—pleasant, unpleasant, or neutral; its roots—physical, physiological, or psychological; and its fruits—physiological, psychological, or social. We can use conscious breathing to assist us in carrying out this work of mindful observation:

Breathing in,
I know that a pleasant feeling has just arisen in me.
Breathing out,
I know that this pleasant feeling is still there.
Breathing in,
I know that this feeling has a psychological basis.
Breathing out,
I can see the roots of this pleasant feeling.
Breathing in,
I can see the influence of this feeling on my health.
Breathing out,
I can see the influence of this feeling on my mind.
And so on.

When roots of affliction such as anger, confusion, jealousy, and anxiety manifest in us, our body and mind are generally disturbed by them. These psychological feelings are unpleasant, and they agitate the functioning of our body and mind. We lose our peace, joy, and calm. In the Sutra on the Full Awareness of Breathing, the Buddha teaches us to take hold of our breathing in order to produce awareness of the unpleasant feeling and gradually to master it: "Breathing in, I know that I have an unpleasant feeling. Breathing out, I am clearly aware of this unpleasant feeling." If our breathing is light and calm (a natural result of practice), then our mind and body will slowly become light, calm, and clear again: "Breathing in, I calm the feelings in me. Breathing out, I calm the feelings in me." In this way, the practitioner continues to use conscious breathing to mindfully observe and calm his feelings. Every time she sees the substance, roots, and effects of her feelings, she is no longer under the control of those feelings. The whole character of our feelings can change just by the presence of mindful observation.

Fear and anger are fields of energy that arise from a physiological or psychological base. The unpleasant feelings that arise within us are also fields of energy. The Buddha teaches us not to repress fear or anger, or the unpleasant feelings brought about by them, but to use our breathing to be in contact with and accept these feelings, knowing that they are energies that originate in our psychological or physiological make-up. To repress our feelings is to repress ourselves. Mindful observation is based on the principle of nonduality. Our unpleasant feelings and ourselves are one. We have to be in contact with and accept the unpleasant feelings before we can transform them into the kinds of energy that are healthy and have the capacity to nourish us. We have to face our unpleasant feelings with care, affection, and nonviolence. Our unpleasant feelings can illuminate so much for us. By our work of mindful observation, we see that experiencing certain unpleasant feelings allows us insight and understanding.

Both in the sutras and the sastras (the commentaries on the sutras), the ancestral teachers say the painful, unpleasant feelings are easier to recognize than the neutral feelings. But in fact, neutral feelings are also easy to recognize. They are not suffering feelings and they are not happy feelings. In us there is a river of feelings, and every drop of water in that river is either a suffering feeling, a happy feeling, or a neutral feeling. Sometimes we have a neutral feeling and we think we don't have a feeling at all. But a neutral feeling is a feeling; it doesn't mean the nonexistence of feeling.

When we have a toothache, we have a feeling of pain, and when the toothache is no longer there, we think we don't have a feeling anymore. But in fact, we have a neutral feeling. It's not a painful feeling, so it must be either neutral or pleasant. Actually, it can be a pleasant feeling. When we have a very bad toothache, we just wish it would stop. We know if it were to stop, we would have a very pleasant feeling. Therefore, a non-toothache is a pleasant feeling. But once the toothache has been gone for some time, we no longer appreciate our non-toothache. We could call it a neutral feeling, but with awareness it can become a pleasant feeling. In Plum Village, we usually say someone who practices mindfulness can change all neutral feelings into pleasant feelings. In fact, neutral feelings are the majority of our feelings.

For example, a father and son are sitting on the lawn in springtime. The father is practicing mindful breathing and he sees how wonderful it is to sit on the grass, feeling fresh and happy, with the yellow flowers coming up and the birds singing; so he has pleasant feelings. But the child is bored, he doesn't want to sit with his father. He's in exactly the same environment as his father. To begin with his feeling is neutral, and at some point the neutral feeling becomes an unpleasant feeling, because he doesn't know how to deal with this neutral feeling. So, wanting to run away from his unpleasant feeling, he stands up and goes into the house and turns on the television. But his father is feeling very content sitting in that same environment that was not able to bring happiness to the son.

We're the same. When we don't have a pleasant or unpleasant feeling, naturally we have a neutral feeling. If we don't know how to deal with or manage our neutral feeling, it will turn into an unpleasant feeling. However, if we know how to manage it, it will become a pleasant feeling, a feeling of well-being. Every neutral feeling, when held in mindfulness, will become a pleasant feeling.

EXERCISES FOR OBSERVING THE MIND

The Third Establishment of Mindfulness presented in the sutra is the establishment of the mind. The contents of the mind are the psychological phenomena called mental formations (*cittasamskara*). Feelings are also mental formations, but they were dealt with on their own in the Second Establishment of Mindfulness, because the sphere of feelings is so wide. What remains are all the other psychological phenomena, such as perceptions, mental formations, and consciousness. These are all mind functions and are the objects of our mindful observation of the mind in the mind. Formations can be either mental, physical, or physiological.

Different schools of Buddhism list different numbers of mental formations. The Abhidharmakosa School lists forty-six, the Satyasiddhi School lists forty-nine, and the Dharmalaksana School lists fifty-one. The Sutra on the Four Establishments of Mindfulness lists only twenty-eight mental formations, including desire, anger, ignorance, disturbance, narrowness, limitedness, lack of concentration, lack of freedom, dullness and drowsiness, agitation and remorse, doubt; their opposites: not-desiring, not-hating, non-ignorance, non-disturbance, tolerance, unlimitedness, concentration, freedom, absence of doubt, absence of dullness and drowsiness, absence of agitation; as well as mindfulness, distaste, peace, joy, ease, and letting go. The second version of the sutra lists one additional mental formation, impurity, which could include other mental formations that are considered to be defilements. The third version considers sensual craving as a formation separate from desire. Any of these mental formations can be the object of our mindful observation of the mind in the mind.

The exercise of observing the mind in the mind isn't different from observing the body in the body or observing the feelings in the feelings. We mindfully observe the arising, presence, and disappearance of the mental phenomena which are called mental formations. We recognize them and look deeply into them in order to see their substance, their roots in the past, and their possible fruits in the future, using conscious breathing while we observe. We should remember that when the lamp of mindfulness is lit up, the mental formation under observation will naturally transform in a wholesome direction.

Exercise 13: Observing the Desiring Mind

> *When his mind is desiring, the practitioner is aware, 'My mind is desiring.' When his mind is not desiring, he is aware, 'My mind is not desiring.' When his mind is hating something,*

he is aware, 'My mind is hating.' When his mind is not hating, he is aware, 'My mind is not hating.' When his mind is in a state of ignorance, he is aware, 'My mind is in a state of ignorance.' When his mind is not in a state of ignorance, he is aware, 'My mind is not in a state of ignorance.' When his mind is tense, he is aware, 'My mind is tense.' When his mind is not tense, he is aware, 'My mind is not tense.' When his mind is distracted, he is aware, 'My mind is distracted.' When his mind is not distracted, he is aware, 'My mind is not distracted.' When his mind has a wider scope, he is aware, 'My mind has widened in scope.' When his mind has a narrow scope, he is aware, 'My mind has become narrow in scope.' When his mind is capable of reaching a higher state, he is aware, 'My mind is capable of reaching a higher state.' When his mind is not capable of reaching a higher state, he is aware, 'My mind is not capable of reaching a higher state.' When his mind is composed, he is aware, 'My mind is composed.' When his mind is not composed, he is aware, 'My mind is not composed.' When his mind is free, he is aware, 'My mind is free.' When his mind is not free, he is aware, 'My mind is not free.'

Desire means to be caught in unwholesome longing. Form, sound, smell, taste, and touch are the objects of the five kinds of sense desire, which are desire for money, sex, fame, good food, and sleep. These five categories of desire produce obstacles on the path of practice as well as many kinds of physical and mental suffering.

Whenever the practitioner's mind and thoughts turn to desiring, she immediately gives rise to awareness of the presence of that mind. "This is a mind longing for wealth. This is a mind of sexual desire. This is a mind desiring reputation. This is the root of the arising of a mind longing for wealth. This is the feeling of pain caused by sexual desire."

The Satipatthana Sutta teaches that when desiring is not present, the practitioner also needs to observe that it is not present. We can practice like this: "At this time, the mind desiring wealth is not present; at this time, sexual desire is not present; at this time, the mind desiring reputation is not present, etc. This is the root of the absence of the desire for wealth. This is the root of the absence of the mind desiring reputation, etc. This is the sense of ease that accompanies the absence of the mind desiring riches. This is the sense of ease that accompanies the absence of a mind desiring reputation, etc."

The Buddha often said that many people confuse desire with happiness. In the Magandiya Sutra (Majjhima Nikaya 75), a man who is forced to live in the forest because he has leprosy, suffering from severe itching and stinging. He dug a hole, filled it with dry branches and logs, and set them on fire. When the fire became red-hot charcoal, he stood at the edge of the hole and stretched his arms and legs out over it to catch the heat. When he did this, his suffering was relieved. On days when he could not make a charcoal fire to warm himself, his itching was unbearable. Miraculously, some years later, he was cured of the disease and went back to live in the village.

One day he went into the forest and saw a number of lepers dragging their bodies to warm themselves by a charcoal fire, and he felt tremendous pity for them. The charcoal was extremely hot, he couldn't go near it. If someone had dragged him to the hole to warm his body over the charcoal, his suffering would have been great. That which in former times had brought him happiness and relief was now a source of agony. The Buddha said, "Desire is also just a hole of burning charcoal in the forest. Only those who are sick look on desire as happiness." Before he became a monk, the Buddha had tasted a life of trying to satisfy the five desires, so his words came from experience. True happiness, he said, is a life with few desires, few possessions, and the time to enjoy the many wonders in us and around us.

The scriptures record how the monk Baddhiya tasted happiness and ease when he observed his life of no desire. One night while sitting in meditation at the foot of a tree in the Bamboo Forest Monastery, Baddhiya suddenly twice called out the words, "O happiness!" The next morning, another bhikkhu reported this to the Buddha, thinking that the monk Baddhiya regretted losing the high position he had had when he was a governor. That afternoon after the Dharma talk, the Buddha summoned Baddhiya and asked, "Is it true that yesterday during your meditation you called out twice, 'O happiness!'?" Baddhiya replied, "Venerable Sir, it is true that last night I called out twice, 'O happiness!'"

"Why?" the Buddha asked him. "Please tell the community."

Baddhiya replied, "Venerable Sir, when I was a governor, I lived in luxury and had great power and influence. Wherever I went, a regiment of soldiers assisted me. My residence was guarded day and night, inside and out, by soldiers. In spite of this, I was always anxious, afraid, and insecure. Now as a bhikkhu, I go into the forest on my own, sit alone at the foot of a tree, sleep alone without a curtain or a mat, and I never have any feelings of unease or fear. I feel a great sense of ease, joy, and peace that I never felt when I was a governor. I do not fear assassins or thieves, because I have nothing to be stolen or fought over. I live at ease like a deer in the forest. During last night's meditation, I felt clearly that feeling of ease, and that is why I raised my voice and called out twice, 'O happiness!' If I disturbed any of my fellow practitioners, I sincerely apologize, Venerable Sir."

The Buddha praised the monk Baddhiya and said to the community, "The monk Baddhiya is making steady and stable progress on the path of contentment and fearlessness. His are the feelings of joy even the gods long for."

In the Vijñanavada school of Buddhist psychology, "desirelessness," the absence of longing for something, is classified as one of the eleven wholesome mental formations. Desirelessness was the basic condition which made possible the feelings of joy, peace, and ease that the monk Baddhiya realized while living the simple life. Simplicity is to have few desires and to be content with just a few possessions. Desirelessness is the basis of true happiness, because in true happiness there must be the elements of peace, joy, and ease.

Exercise 14: Observing Anger

> *When anger is present in him, he is aware, 'Anger is present in me.' When anger is not present in him, he is aware, 'Anger is not present in me.' When anger begins to arise, he is aware of it. When already arisen anger is abandoned, he is aware of it. When anger already abandoned will not arise again in the future, he is aware of it.*

This exercise is to observe our anger in mindfulness. In Buddhism, we learn that a person is comprised of the Five Aggregates of form, feelings, perceptions, mental formations, and consciousness. Anger belongs to the aggregate of mental formations, and the unpleasant feeling that goes along with the anger belongs to the aggregate of feelings. The mastery of our anger is an important step on the path of practice. Identifying the presence and the absence of anger in us brings many benefits. For our work of mindful observation to be wholehearted, we combine the work of observation with conscious breathing.

The first benefit of mindfully observing the presence and absence of anger is that we see that when anger is not present, we are much happier. Anger is like a flame blazing up and consuming our self-control, making us think, say, and do things that we will probably regret later. The actions of body, speech, and mind that we perform while we're angry take us a long way along the road to hell. We may never have seen the Avici hells, but we can see clearly that whenever someone is angry, he is abiding in one of the hot hells. Anger and hatred are the materials of which the Avici hells are made. A mind without anger—cool, fresh, and sane—is one of the eleven wholesome mental formations. The absence of anger is the basis of real happiness, the basis of love and compassion.

The second benefit of mindfully observing the presence and absence of anger is that by just identifying our anger, it loses some of its destructive nature. Only when we're angry and not observing our anger mindfully does our anger become destructive. When anger is born in us, we should follow our breathing closely while we identify and mindfully observe our anger. When we do that, mindfulness has already been born in us, and anger can no longer monopolize our consciousness. Awareness stands alongside the anger: "I know that I am angry." This awareness is a companion for the anger. Our mindful observation is not to suppress or drive out our anger, but just to look after it. This is a very important principle in meditation practice. Mindful observation is like a lamp that gives light. It's not a judge. It throws light on our anger, sponsors it, looks after it in an affectionate and caring way, like an older sister looking after and comforting her younger sibling.

When we're angry, our anger is our very self. To suppress or chase away our anger is to suppress or chase away ourselves. When we're joyful, we are joy. When we're angry, we are anger. When we love, we are love. When we hate, we are hatred. When anger is born, we can be aware that anger is an energy in us, and we can change that energy into another kind of energy. If we want to transform it, first we have to know how to accept it. For example, a garbage can filled with decomposing and smelly organic material can be transformed into compost and later into beautiful roses. At first, we may see the garbage and the flowers as separate and opposite, but when we look deeply, we see that the flowers already exist in the garbage, and the garbage already exists in the flowers. The beautiful rose contains the garbage in it; if we look carefully, we can see that. It only takes one week for a flower to become garbage. The smelly garbage already contains beautiful flowers and fragrant herbs, such as coriander and basil. When a good organic gardener looks into the garbage can, she can see that, and so she does not feel sad or disgusted. Instead, she values the garbage and doesn't discriminate against it. It takes only a few months for garbage to transform into fragrant herbs and flowers. We also need the insight and nondual vision of the organic gardener with regard to anger and despair. We need not be afraid of them or reject them. We know that anger is a kind of garbage, but that it's within our power to transform it. We need it in the way the organic gardener needs compost. If we know how to accept our anger, we already have some peace and joy. Gradually we can transform anger completely.

When anger arises, other mental formations, which are lying latent in the depths of our consciousness, are not arising. This deep consciousness is called *alaya* by the Vijñanavada school. Joy, sadness, love, and hate, for example, are present in alaya when we are angry, but they are lying beneath the surface without manifesting, like seeds (Sanskrit: *bija*) in the ground. If we let the anger express itself without giving it a sponsor, it can do a lot of damage inside and outside of us. When the mental formation mindfulness arises from alaya, it can become the spiritual friend of the mental formation anger. As we follow our breathing and sponsor our anger with mindfulness, the situation becomes less and less dangerous. Although the anger is still there, it gradually loses its strength and begins to transform into another kind of energy, like love or understanding.

Mindfulness is like a lamp illuminating ourselves. As soon as the lamp is brought into the room, the room changes. When the sun rises, the light of the sun only has to shine onto the plants for them to change, grow, and develop. The light of the sun appears not to be doing anything at all, but in truth it is doing a lot. Under the influence of the sun, the plants produce chlorophyll and become green. It is thanks to the growth of plants that the animal species have what they need to survive. If the sun keeps shining on the bud, the flower will open. When the light of the sun penetrates the flower bud, the photons transform it, and the flower opens. Our mindfulness has the same function as the light of the sun. If we shine the light of full awareness steadily on our state of mind, that state of mind will transform into something better.

Thanks to the illuminating light of awareness, we can see the roots of our anger. The point of meditation is to look deeply into things in order to be able to see their nature. The nature of things is interdependent origination, the true source of everything that is. If we look into our anger, we can see its roots, such as misunderstanding (or ignorance), clumsiness (or lack of skill), the surrounding society, hidden resentment, and habit (or our conditioning). These roots can be present both in ourselves and in the person who played the principal role in allowing the anger to arise. We observe mindfully in order to be able to see and to understand. Seeing and understanding are the elements of liberation that allow us to be free of the suffering which always accompanies anger. Seeing and understanding bring about love and compassion. They are the balm of the bodhisattva's compassion that cools our hearts and mind. As we have already seen, our anger is a field of energy. Thanks to our mindful observation and insight into its roots, we can change this energy into the energy of love and compassion—a constructive and healing energy.

Usually when people are angry, they say and do things that cause damage to others and themselves. There are people who speak and act in ways that wound others. They believe that doing so will release the field of angry energy that is burning in their hearts. They shout and scream, beat things, and shoot poisoned arrows of speech at others. These methods of release are dangerous.

Sometimes people try to find ways to express their anger in a less dangerous way. They may go into their room, close the door behind them, and pound a pillow with all their might. Naturally if you beat a pillow until your energy is exhausted, your anger will subside, and you'll probably experience a temporary feeling of relief—exhaustion is easier to bear than anger—but the roots of the anger remain untouched, and when the conditions are right, the same anger will arise again. Therefore, the method of mindful observation in order to see and to understand the roots of our anger is the only method that has lasting effectiveness.

As we've seen already, when anger arises, we first need to come back to our conscious breathing and sponsor our anger with mindfulness. We concentrate on our breathing in order to maintain mindfulness. We avoid listening to or looking at the person whom we regard as the cause of our anger. Usually when we're angry, we don't return to ourselves and take care of healing our anger. We want to think about the hateful aspects of the person who has made us angry—rudeness, dishonesty, cruelty, maliciousness, and so on. The more we think of them, listen to them, or look at them, the more our anger flares up. Their hatefulness may be real, imaginary, or exaggerated, but whatever it is that's making us angry, we're inclined to give our full attention to that. In fact, the root of our problem is the anger inside of us, and we have to come back to it and take care of it first of all. Like a firefighter, we must put water on the blaze immediately and not waste time looking for the person who set the house on fire. "Breathing in, I know that I am angry. Breathing out, I know that I must take care of my anger."

So it's best not to listen to, look at, or think about the other person, or to say or do anything as long as anger persists. If we put our mind into the work of observing and calming our anger, we'll avoid creating damage that we would probably regret later. We may like to go outside and practice walking meditation. The fresh air, green trees, and the plants will help us greatly. As we walk, we can recite this verse:

> Breathing in, I know that anger is still here.
> Breathing out, I know that anger is me.
> And I know that mindfulness is me also.
> Breathing in, I know that anger is an unpleasant feeling.
> Breathing out, I know that this feeling has been born and will die.
> Breathing in, I know that I can take care of this feeling.
> Breathing out, I calm this feeling.

Mindfulness embraces the feeling, as a mother holds her crying child in her arms and transmits all her affection and care. If a mother puts all her heart and mind into caring for her baby, the baby will feel the mother's gentleness and will calm down. In the same way, we can calm the functioning of our mind.

In order to lessen the unpleasant feeling brought about by the anger, we give our whole heart and mind to the practice of walking meditation, combining our breath with our steps and giving full attention to the contact between the soles of our feet and the earth. After a while, our anger will calm down, and we become stronger. Then we can begin to observe the anger and its true nature.

We know that we can't eat potatoes without cooking them first. We fill our pot with water, put the lid on, and light the fire. The lid of the pot, which keeps the heat inside, is the power of concentration—not to speak, not to listen, not to do anything at all, but just to concentrate our whole mind on our breathing. As soon as the pot is on the fire, the water begins to get warm. When we practice conscious breathing, although our anger is still there, it's accompanied by mindfulness, the fire under the potatoes. The anger—the potatoes—has started to transform. Half an hour later, the potatoes are cooked, and our anger is transformed. We can smile, and we know that we understand the roots of our anger, and we can face the person who precipitated it.

Our anger is rooted in our lack of understanding of ourselves and of the causes, deep-seated as well as immediate, which have brought about this unpleasant state of affairs. Anger is also rooted in desire, pride, agitation, and suspiciousness. Our method of dealing with events as they arise reflects our state of understanding as well as our state of confusion. The chief roots of our anger are in ourselves. Our environment and other people are only secondary roots.

We can put up with the damage brought about by an earthquake or a flood, but if people had caused the same damage, we might not show much patience, and anger and hatred may arise in us. But if we know that earthquakes and floods have causes, we should also be able to see that there are causes—deep-seated or immediate—of the harm done to us by people. We need to see and understand these causes also. We have to see hardships brought about by others as a sort of natural disaster. These people make our lives difficult because they're ignorant, prisoners of their desires or their hatreds. If we speak angrily to them and treat them as our enemy, then we're just doing what they are doing, and we're no different from them. In order to realize the state of no anger in our conscious and subconscious mind, we have to practice the meditations on love and compassion.

Exercise 15: Love Meditation

When anger is not present in him, he is aware, 'Anger is not present in me.' When already arisen anger is abandoned, he is aware of it. When anger already abandoned will not arise again in the future, he is aware of it ... When his mind is not attached, he is aware, 'My mind is not attached.' When his mind is not hating, he is aware, 'My mind is not hating.'

In the Anguttara Nikaya (V, 161), the Buddha teaches, "If a mind of anger arises, the bhikkhu can practice the meditation on love, on compassion, or on equanimity for the person who has brought about the feeling of anger." Love meditation is a method for developing the mind of love and compassion. Love (Pali: *metta*; Sanskrit: *maitri*) is a mind that is intent on bringing peace, joy, and happiness to others. Compassion (Sanskrit: *karuna*) is a mind that is intent on removing the suffering which is present in others. That is the meaning of the phrase, "Love is the capacity to give joy. Compassion is the power to relieve suffering." When love and compassion are sources of energy in us, they bring peace, joy, and happiness to those dear to us and to others also.

We all have the seeds of love and compassion in us, and we can develop these fine and wonderful sources of energy. Maitri and karuna aren't the kinds of love that try to possess and appropriate, to dictate and bring about suffering for ourselves and those we love. Maitri and karuna are the kinds of unconditional love that don't expect anything in return. Consequently they don't result in anxiety, boredom, or sorrow.

The essence of love and compassion is understanding, the ability to recognize the suffering of others. We have to be in touch with the physical, material, and psychological suffering of others. To do so, we have to put ourselves "inside the skin" of the other. We must "go inside" their body, feelings, and mental formations and experience their suffering. A shallow observation as an outsider won't help us see their suffering. In the Satipatthana Sutta, we're taught to be one with the object of our observation. We observe the body in the body, the feelings in the feelings, the mental formations in the mental formations.

When we're in contact with the suffering of another, a feeling of compassion is born in us immediately. Compassion literally means "to suffer with" the other. Looking in order to see the suffering in another person is the work of meditation. If we sit cross-legged, follow our breathing, and observe someone mindfully, we can be in contact with his suffering, and the energy of compassion arises in us. We can also do this while walking, standing, lying down, sitting, speaking, and acting, not just when we are sitting in meditation. The physical and psychological suffering of that person will be clear to us in the light of our mindful observation.

When the mind of compassion arises, we have to find ways to nourish and express it. When we come into contact with the other person, our thoughts and actions should express our mind of compassion, even if that person says and does things that are not easy to accept. We practice in this way until we see clearly that our love is not contingent upon the other person apologizing or being lovable. Then we can be sure that our mind of compassion is firm and authentic. We'll recognize in ourselves some of the beautiful signs of the compassionate mind: (1) our sleep is more relaxed, (2) we do not have nightmares, (3) our waking-state is more at ease, (4) we're not anxious or depressed, and (5) we're protected by everyone and everything around us. The person who has been the object of our meditation on compassion will also, eventually, benefit from our meditation. His suffering will slowly diminish, and his life will gradually be brighter and more joyful.

We can begin our meditation on compassion with someone who is undergoing suffering of a physical or material kind—someone who is weak and easily ill, poor, or oppressed, or has no protection. This kind of suffering is easy to see. We observe it deeply, either during sitting meditation or when we're actually in contact with it. We must have enough time if we're going to be in deep contact with the suffering of that person. We have to observe until the mind of compassion arises, and the substance of the mind of compassion penetrates into our being. Then the mind of compassion will envelop the object of our observation. If we observe deeply in this way, the mind of compassion will naturally be transformed into action. We won't just say, "I love her very much," but instead, "I must do something so that she'll suffer less." The mind of compassion is truly present when it has the capacity of removing suffering.

After that, we can practice being in contact with more subtle forms of suffering. Sometimes the other person doesn't seem to be suffering at all, but we may notice that she has sorrows which have left their marks in hidden ways. Someone with more than enough material comforts can also be subject to suffering. There are very few people who are not suffering to some degree. The person who has made us suffer is undoubtedly suffering too. We only need to sit down, follow our breathing, and look deeply, and naturally we'll see her suffering.

We may be able to see how her misery has come about because of the lack of skill of the parents who raised her. But her parents may have been the victims of their parents. The suffering has been transmitted from generation to generation, and it has been reborn in her. If we can see that, we'll no longer blame her for making us suffer, because we understand the way in which she is also a victim. To look deeply is to understand. Once we understand, it's easy to embrace the other person in our mind of compassion.

To look deeply into the suffering of those who have caused us to suffer is a miraculous gift. Thanks to our observation, we now know that the person is suffering. He may think that his suffering will be lessened if he can cause us to suffer. Once we're in touch with his suffering, our enmity and bitterness towards him will vanish, and we'll long for him to suffer less. The spring water of the compassionate mind begins to flow, and we ourselves are the first to be cleansed by it. We feel cool and light, and we can smile. We don't need two people to bring about reconciliation. When we look deeply, we become reconciled with ourselves and, for us, the problem no longer exists. Sooner or later, the other will see our attitude and share in the freshness of the stream of love which is flowing naturally in our heart.

After we experience the fruit of the meditation of compassion, the meditation on love becomes relatively easy. Just as with the mind of compassion, the mind of love brings peace, joy, and happiness to the practitioner first. We know that if we don't have peace and joy ourselves, we won't have peace and joy to share with others. That's why the meditation on compassion and the meditation on love bring benefits both to the practitioner and to others.

When we reduce the suffering in others, we also bring them happiness at the same time. Although life is suffering, it also has many wonderful things like the early morning sky, the harvest moon, the forsythia bush, the violet bamboo, the stream of clear water, and the beautiful child. When we pay attention only to our suffering, we're not able to make contact with these wonderful things, and anything we say or do will not untie the knot of suffering and bring about the conditions for living joyfully. Mindful observation is the element that nourishes the tree of understanding, and compassion and love are the most beautiful flowers. When we realize the mind of love, we have to go to the one who has been the object of our mindful observation, so that our mind of love is not just an object of our imagination but is a source of energy that has an effect in the real world.

The Buddha teaches that during our meditation we can send our mind of love and compassion into the four directions and embrace all species of living beings. But we must be careful not to think that the meditations of love and compassion consist in just sitting still and imagining that our mind of love and compassion will spread out into space like waves of sound or light. Sound and light have the ability to penetrate everywhere, and love and compassion can do the same. But if our love and compassion are only a kind of imagining—for example, if we imagine they are like a pure white cloud that slowly forms and gradually spreads out and out to envelop the whole world—then they'll have no effect; they're only a cloud of the imagination. A true cloud can produce rain. It's only in the midst of our daily life and in our actual contact with people and other species, including the object of our meditation, that we can know whether our mind of love and compassion is really present and whether it is stable. If love and compassion are real, they'll be evident in our daily life, in the way we talk with people and the way we act in the world. The sitting meditation position is not the only position in which we can give rise to the spring water of love and compassion.

Many people think that if they don't have influence and money, they can't realize love and compassion. In fact, the source of love and compassion is in us, and we can help many people suffer less and realize a lot of happiness without being rich or influential. One word, one action, or one thought can reduce another person's suffering and bring him joy. One word can give comfort and confidence, destroy doubt, help someone avoid a mistake, reconcile a conflict, open the door to liberation, or show him the way to success and happiness. One action can save a person's life or help him take advantage of a rare opportunity. One thought can do the same, because thoughts lead to words and action. If love and compassion are in our hearts, every thought, word, and deed can bring about a miracle. Because understanding is the very foundation of love and compassion, the words and actions engendered by love and compassion will be ones that are helpful. When we want to help, we know how to avoid the kind of love that does more harm than good. We must always remember that love is none other than understanding.

EXERCISES FOR OBSERVING THE OBJECTS OF MIND

Exercise 16: Discriminative Investigation

> *When the factor of awakening, investigation-of-phenomena, is present in him, he is aware, 'Investigation-of-phenomena is present in me.' He is aware when not-yet-born investigation-of-phenomena is being born and when already-born investigation-of-phenomena is perfectly developed.*

Ignorance, or delusion, is the erroneous perception of things. In order to correct our erroneous perceptions, the Buddha teaches us a method of discriminative investigation, which relates to the establishment of the mind and the establishment of the objects of mind. The objects of mind are also called dharmas (all that can be conceived of as existing). They include the six sense organs, the six sense objects, and the six sense consciousnesses. The six sense organs are the eyes, ears, nose, tongue, body, and mind. The six sense objects are form and color, sound, smell, taste, tactile objects, and mind-objects (every concept and every thing that belongs to the sphere of memory and mental experience). The sense six consciousnesses are: eye-consciousness (or sight), ear-consciousness (or hearing), nose-consciousness (or smelling), taste-consciousness (or tasting), body-consciousness (or touching), and mind-consciousness. All dharmas are contained within these Eighteen Realms (Sanskrit: *dhatu*), which include all psychological, physiological, and physical aspects. All Eighteen Realms are also called objects of mind, including mental formations. When mind is observing mind, the mind becomes an object of mind.

The basic characteristic of all dharmas is interdependent origination. All dharmas arise, endure, and fade away according to the law of interdependence. In the Majjhima Nikaya, it is taught: "This is, because that is; this is not, because that is not. This is produced, because that is produced. This is destroyed, because that is destroyed." The Buddhist principle of interdependence, put forward with the utmost simplicity, is immeasurably deep. According to this teaching, no single dharma can arise by itself, endure by itself, and fade away by itself. The coming-to-be of one dharma is dependent on the coming-to-be, endurance, and destruction of other dharmas, in fact, of all other dharmas. Dharmas do not have independent existence. They're empty of a separate, independent existence.

In our daily life, we're inclined to perceive things as real and independent of each other. Take, for example, a leaf we see on the branch in front of us. We may think that this leaf exists independently of all the other leaves, independently of the branch, the trunk, and the roots of the tree; independently of the clouds, the water, the earth, and the sky. In truth, this leaf could not be here without the presence of all the other things that we see as different from it. This leaf is one with the other leaves, the branch, the trunk, and the roots of the tree; with the clouds, the river, the earth, the sky, and the sunlight. If any one of these things were not present, the leaf could not be. If we look deeply into the leaf, we can see the presence of all these things. The leaf and these things are present together. This is the principle of interbeing and interpenetration, the principle of one is all and all is one, which the Avatamsaka Sutra, the most complete and sufficient expression of the Buddhist principle of interdependent origination, teaches. Things do not exist outside of each other. Things exist within each other and with each other. That is why the Buddha said: "This is, because that is." With the power of concentration, we can observe all that is in the light of this principle. All phenomena in the universe, including the thoughts, words, and feelings of both ourselves and those around us, need to be observed in the light of interdependence.

This method of discriminative investigation begins by classifying the dharmas into categories like the six sense organs, the six sense objects, and the six sense consciousnesses, namely, the Eighteen Realms, which can also be classified according to the Five Aggregates of form, feeling, perceptions, mental formations, and consciousness. By "form," we mean all physiological and physical phenomena. "Feelings" means pleasant, unpleasant, and neutral feelings. "Perceptions" means basic conceptualizations and naming. "Mental formations" means psychological states that arise and manifest in us. "Consciousness" is the function of maintaining, cognizing, comparing, storing, and remembering all the seeds. The basic Abhidharma writings and the teachings of the Vijñanavada school of Buddhist psychology give very thorough explanations of the essential nature of these five categories and the ways in which they function.

The Heart of the Prajñaparamita Sutra tells us that the Bodhisattva Avalokita, thanks to his observation of the Five Aggregates, was able to see the interdependent nature of all dharmas and realize their essential birthlessness and deathlessness, and so transcend the fear of birth and death. The same sutra refers to the essential emptiness (Sanskrit: *sunyata*) of all dharmas. Emptiness, here, means interdependence. All dharmas depend on each other in order to arise and to endure. There is no dharma which can exist apart from other dharmas, and that is why we say that the real nature of dharmas is emptiness. Nothing can exist on its own.

Through discriminative investigation, we realize the interdependent nature of all that is. This is to realize the empty nature of all things.

With insight into emptiness, we'll go beyond concepts of "it is" and "it is not," birth and death, one and many, coming and going, and we'll transcend the fear of birth and death. Our concepts of it is/it is not, birth/death, one/many, coming/going, and so on, will dissolve when we're witness to the interdependent nature of all that is. To be able to end the concept of birth and death is the essential point of discriminative investigation.

Some days before the layman Anathapindika passed away, the Buddha sent the Venerable Sariputra and the Venerable Ananda to visit him and instruct him in his practice. Sitting at the layman's bedside, the Venerable Sariputra began his instruction: "Layman Anathapindika, you should meditate like this: 'These eyes are not me. I am not caught in these eyes.'" Anathapindika breathed and meditated according to the instructions. Sariputra continued his instructions: "These ears, nose, tongue, body, and mind are not me. I am not caught by forms, sounds, smells, tastes, contacts, or the thoughts that I have." Anathapindika observed in this way in order to see gradually the interdependent nature of all that is, to see that he himself was not restricted to the Eighteen Realms (the six sense organs, the six sense objects, and the six sense consciousnesses), and to see that there's no birth that brings us into existence and no death that takes us from existence to nonexistence.

When he had practiced this much, Anathapindika began to weep, the tears falling down his cheeks. The Venerable Ananda asked, "What is it? Do you regret anything? Did you not succeed in the meditation?" Anathapindika replied, "Venerable Ananda, I have nothing to regret, and my meditation has been very successful. I'm crying because I am so moved. I have been lucky enough to have served the Buddha and his community for many years, but I have never heard a teaching so deep, so wonderful, and so precious as the teaching transmitted by the Venerable Sariputra today."

"Layman Anathapindika, do you not know that the Buddha is always giving this teaching to monks and nuns?" Ananda said.

"Venerable Ananda, please tell the Buddha that laypersons such as myself could also listen to this wonderful teaching. There are laypeople who are too busy to hear, understand, and put into practice these wonderful and deep teachings, but there are also laypeople with the capacity to listen, understand, and put into practice these wonderful and deep teachings."

This excerpt about the layman Anathapindika (Majjhima Nikaya 143) shows us that anyone can practice the mindful observation of the interdependent and empty nature of things, not just monks or nuns. The life of a layperson is not so busy that he is not able to enjoy the taste of the highest teachings of Buddhism.

The Sutra on the Four Establishments of Mindfulness also describes the mind that is not in a state of ignorance and confusion, as when we are conscious of impermanence, interdependence, and selflessness; when our mind rests in Right View. Right View is one of the eight ways of practice called the Noble Eightfold Path.

In the section that teaches how to be mindful of the objects of mind, among the Seven Factors of Awakening (Sanskrit: *saptabodhyanga*), the investigation of dharmas is mentioned. Investigation of dharmas means the detailed examination of the source and the nature of phenomena whether physical or psychological. Investigation of dharmas has a meaning similar to discriminative investigation and is also intended to see the source and the nature of dharmas. If we can understand in depth the source and the nature of dharmas, then our mind is not in a state of ignorance or confusion.

Each of the above fifteen exercises from the Satipatthana Sutta has, to a greater or lesser degree, the function of mindfully observing the source of dharmas. The most obvious examples are the eighth exercise—observation of the interdependence of the body and all that is in the universe: earth, water, air, and fire—and the twelfth exercise—the observation of the source and the nature of our feelings.

When sitting in meditation, we concentrate our mind on the object of our observation—sometimes a physical phenomenon, sometimes psychological—and we look deeply into that object in order to discover its source and its nature. The role of our conscious breathing is to nourish and maintain our power of concentration on one object. If we look carefully and deeply, naturally we'll see that the arising, enduring, and ending of the object is dependent on other things. Eventually we'll see that the true nature of all dharmas is birthlessness and deathlessness, and that although dharmas are not everlasting, they're never totally destroyed. Thus the mindful observation of interdependence is the road that leads us to transcend the limits of birth and death. A student of Buddhism who doesn't practice the mindful observation of interdependence hasn't yet arrived at the quintessence of the Buddhist path.

Exercise 17: Observing Internal Formations

> He is aware of the eyes [ears, nose, tongue, body, mind] and aware of the form [sound, smell, taste, touch, objects of mind], and he is aware of the internal formations which are produced in dependence on these two things. He is aware of the birth of a new internal formation and is aware of abandoning an already produced internal formation, and he

is aware when an already abandoned internal formation will not arise again.

In the section of the sutra that refers to the observation of the six sense organs and the six sense objects, we see the term "internal formations." The word in Sanskrit is *samyojana*, which can also be translated as "knots," "fetters," "agglomeration," or "binding together."

Internal formations can be classified as two kinds, the Five Dull Knots: confusion, desire, anger, pride, and doubt; and the Five Sharp Knots: view of the body as self, extreme views, wrong views, perverted views, and superstitious views (or unnecessary ritual prohibitions). The latter are easier to correct. When the eyes see form, the ears hear sound, the nose smells a scent, the tongue tastes something, the body touches something, or the mind cognizes an object, knots may or may not be tied, depending on the way in which our mind receives these impressions. When someone speaks unkindly to us, if we understand the reason and we do not take the words to heart, we won't feel at all irritated, and a knot won't be formed in our mind. If we don't understand the reason and we feel irritated, a knot will form. The substance of this knot will be hatred. When we misunderstand someone's words or behavior, the knot that forms is confusion, which often gives rise to irritation, pride, attachment, and doubt. The knot of confusion, a lack of clear seeing, or ignorance

(Sanskrit: *avidya*), is the basis for every other knot.

The feelings associated with internal formations are usually unpleasant, but sometimes internal formations are associated with pleasant feelings. When we are attached to a form, sound, scent, taste, touch, or mind object, an internal formation of the nature of desire is formed. To begin with, it can be associated with a pleasant feeling. But because we become attached to it, we are bound, and when the demands of the attachment are not met, the feelings become unpleasant. Anything from wine, tobacco, or opium to beautiful forms, good food, music, or words of praise can produce a knot in us, an internal formation that begins as a pleasant feeling. Once we have a such a knot, we are tied tightly by it, and we are forced to seek out the object of sense again and again in order to repeat the pleasant feeling.

Falling in love is also an internal formation, because in it there is the material of blind attachment. The term to "fall" in love in itself sounds disastrous. People often refer to love-sickness, as if falling in love were a disease. The French expression *coup de foudre* (struck by lightning) describes falling in love as a sharp blow. The author Nguyên Bính has said, "Alas, only the gods can save someone who has fallen in love." But being in love can be transformed, so that blind attachment, selfishness, and domination are replaced by the capacity to understand and bring happiness to the person we love, without demanding specific conditions and expecting something in return. To transform being in love in this way is to transform an internal formation.

Feelings of sorrow in us are also internal formations that arise from confusion, desire, hatred, pride, and doubt. If these roots of affliction are not transformed, the feelings of sorrow will remain intact in us. In everyday life, seeds of sorrow can be sown in our consciousness with or without the collaboration of others. Others may say or do things that produce knots in us, but if we give birth to the seeds of understanding, tolerance, love, and compassion, then what they say and do will not produce any internal formations in us. It depends on the way in which we receive what happens to us in our daily lives. If we are stable, relaxed, understanding, loving, compassionate, and not caught in egotism, then the things others do and say will not have the force to produce an internal formation in us.

If we live according to the teachings of the Four Establishments of Mindfulness, we practice mindful observation of the arising, duration, and transformation of internal formations. In our daily life, we practice full awareness in order to be able to recognize the internal formation just born and find a way to transform it. If we allow internal formations to grow strong in us, the time will come when they will dominate us, and the work of transforming them will be extremely difficult. An internal formation of hatred, desire, or doubt needs our full attention as soon as it arises so that it may be transformed. When it arises for the first time, the knot is still very "loose" and the work of "untying it" is easy.

When we live with another person, we should help each other transform the internal formations that we have produced in each other. By practicing understanding and loving speech, we can help each other a great deal. Happiness is no longer an individual matter. If the other person is not happy, we will not be happy either. Therefore, to transform the internal formations in the other is to bring about our own happiness as well. A person can create internal formations in her partner, and her partner can do so for her, and if they continue to create knots in each other, one day they'll have no happiness left. A person needs to recognize quickly any newly formed knot inside herself. She should take the time to observe it and, with her partner's help, transform the internal formation. She might say, "Darling, I have an internal formation. Can you please help me?" This is easy when the states of mind of both partners are still light and not loaded with many internal formations.

As we have already seen, the material of any internal formation is ignorance or confusion. If we can see the ignorance that is present during the creation of a knot, we can easily untie it. In the twelfth exercise (mindfully observing the source and nature of feelings), the fourteenth exercise (mindfully observing anger), and the fifteenth exercise (observing with compassion), we have seen that if we're aware of interdependence and multiple causation, we can see the roots and the nature of our mind and transform and transcend unpleasant states. Mindful observation is to look and be able to see the nature of dharmas. The transformation of an internal formation is the result of this insight.

Exercise 18: Transforming Internal Formations

> *He is aware of the eyes [ears, nose, tongue, body, mind] and aware of the form [sound, smell, taste, touch, objects of mind], and he is aware of the internal formations which are produced in dependence on these two things. He is aware of the birth of a new internal formation and is aware of abandoning an already produced internal formation, and he is aware when an already abandoned internal formation will not arise again.* [This is the same quote as in Exercise 17.]

This exercise aims at putting us in touch with and transforming internal formations that are buried and repressed in ourselves. The internal formations of desire, anger, fear, feeling worthless, and regret have been suppressed in our subconscious for a long time. Although they are suppressed, they are always seeking ways to manifest in our feelings, thoughts, words, and actions. It is easy for us to observe our internal formations when they appear as feelings on the surface of consciousness, but internal formations that are repressed cannot appear in a direct and natural way in the conscious mind. They only disclose themselves indirectly. Thus we're not aware of their presence, although they continue to tie us up and make us suffer in a latent way.

What is it that represses them and does not let them appear? It is our conscious, reasoning mind. We know that our desires and anger are not wholly acceptable to society and to our own reasoning mind, so we've found a way to repress them, to push them into remote areas of our consciousness in order to be able to forget them. This is the work of a mental formation called *mushita smrti*, forgetfulness. Contemporary psychology understands repression. Because we want to avoid suffering, there are defense mechanisms in us that push our psychological pains, conflicts, and unacceptable desires into our unconscious so that we can feel more at peace with ourselves. But our longstanding repressions are always looking for ways to manifest in words, images, and behavior unacceptable to society and can later become symptoms of physical and psychological illness. We may know that our words, thoughts, and behavior are destructive, but we can't do anything about them because our internal formations are so strong.

Take for example a daughter who, on the one hand, wants to be with a partner or do her own things in the world, and on the other hand does not want to leave her mother to live all alone. The daughter understands and loves her mother, but she also wants to be independent and/or live with the person she loves. However, her mother is sick and needs someone to support her, and the daughter can't bear the thought of leaving her alone. The opposing desires and feelings bring about an internal conflict in the daughter. And so her defense mechanism represses the pain of the conflict in her unconscious and tells her to devote her life to supporting her mother. Nevertheless, the desire to be with her own partner is still there, and the psychological conflict remains an internal formation looking for a way to manifest. She becomes irritable and says things which even she herself does not understand, and she has dreams which are incomprehensible to her. She is not happy, and so her mother can't be happy either. In fact, her mother has been haunted for years by the fear that her daughter will leave her, and it is this psychological factor that made her unexpectedly fall sick and grow weak, although she's not aware of it. When she heard her daughter say that she was going to stay, she was very pleased, but in the depths of her heart, she suffers because she knows that her daughter is prevented from doing something she wants to do. This conflict becomes an internal formation in the mother, which makes her suffer, and the mother also becomes irritable and says things which she herself does not understand. She also has dreams she doesn't understand, and she does things without knowing why she's doing them. Neither the mother nor the daughter is happy, and both continue to suffer.

The method of curing the sorrow that comes when internal formations are repressed is the deep observation of these internal formations. But to observe them, first of all we have to find ways to bring them into the realm of the conscious mind. The method of the Sutra on the Four Establishments of Mindfulness is to practice conscious breathing in order to recognize our feelings, thoughts, words, and actions, especially those which arise automatically, as reactions to what is happening. Our reactions may have their roots in the internal formations buried inside us.

When we're aware of what we are feeling, thinking, and doing, we can ask ourselves questions like: Why do I feel uncomfortable when I hear someone say that? Why do I always think of my mother when I see that woman? Why did I say that to him? Why didn't I like that character in the film? Whom did I hate in the past who this person resembles? Practices like this can help us discover the roots of our feelings, thoughts, words, and behavior and gradually bring the internal formations buried in us into the realm of the conscious mind.

During our sitting meditation, because we have closed the doors of our sensory input in order to stop listening, looking, and reasoning, the internal formations that are buried in us have the opportunity to reveal themselves in the form of feelings or images that manifest in our conscious mind. To begin with, there may be just a feeling of anxiety, fear, or unpleasantness, whose cause we can't see. We have to shine the light of mindfulness on it and be ready to see this feeling.

When this feeling begins to show its face and to gather strength and become more intense, we may feel it robs us of all our peace, joy, and ease. We may not want to be in contact with it anymore. We may want to move our attention to another object of meditation. We may not want to continue with the meditation, and we may say that we're sleepy and would prefer to meditate some other time. In modern psychology, this is called resistance. Deep down we are afraid to bring into our conscious mind the feelings of pain that are buried within us, because they'll make us suffer.

There are people who practice sitting meditation many hours a day, but they do not really dare to face and invite their feelings of pain into their conscious mind. They deceive themselves that these feelings aren't important and they give their attention to other subjects of meditation—impermanence, selflessness, the sound of one hand clapping, or the reason

Bodhidharma came to the West. This isn't to suggest that these subjects are unimportant, but they should be considered in the light of our real problems in order to be authentic subjects for meditation practice.

We don't practice mindfulness in Buddhism in order to repress our feelings, but as a way of looking after our feelings, being their sponsor in an affectionate, nonviolent way. When we're able to maintain mindfulness, we're not carried away by or drowned in our feelings or in the conflicts within ourselves. We nourish and maintain mindfulness through conscious breathing and try to become aware of our internal formations and conflicts as they manifest. We receive them with love as a mother takes her child in her arms: "Mindfulness is present, and I know that I have enough strength to be in contact with the knots in me." In this kind of an environment, our internal formations will manifest as feelings and images in our mind that we can contact and identify fully and deeply.

Without judgment, blame, or criticism for having these feelings or images, we just observe, identify, and accept them in order to see their source and their true nature. If there's pain, we feel the pain. If there's sadness, we are sad. If there's anger, then we are angry, but our anger is accompanied by mindfulness. We don't lose ourselves in the pain, the sadness, or the anger, but we calm them down. Even if we haven't seen the roots of the internal formations, the fact that we can greet our pain, our sadness, and our anger in mindfulness already causes our internal knots to lose some of their strength. Thanks to our vigilant observation, eventually we'll see their roots and transform them. The teaching of the Sutra on the Four Establishments of Mindfulness on how to be in direct contact with our feelings and invite them up to manifest on the surface of our consciousness is wonderfully effective. The practitioner can work with difficult internal formations with the help of a teacher or of a co-practitioner. The teacher and the co-practitioners, because of their mindful observation, can help point out to him the manifestations of the internal formations that lie deep in his consciousness.

In his lifetime, the Buddha was praised as being a King of Doctors, and he helped thousands of people, including King Ajatasatru of Magadha, deal with mental problems. Those who practice mindful observation can learn the Buddhist way of dealing with internal formations in order to help themselves and others. Because many people live without practicing mindfulness and don't know how to transform internal formations, over time these internal formations become strong and lead to agitation, anxiety, and depression, which express themselves in speech and behavior that are not easily acceptable by society. Those with strong internal formations have difficulty relating to and working with others, and these difficulties make them feel more and more unsuccessful in society. As their internal formations increase, their behavior becomes more and more inappropriate, and eventually, the pressure may become so great that they'll have to quit their job or abandon their marriage.

If we know how to live every moment in an awakened way, we'll be aware of what's happening in our feelings and perceptions in the present moment and won't let internal formations become too tight in our consciousness. If we know how to observe our feelings, we can find the causes of longstanding internal formations and transform them.

Exercise 19: Overcoming Guilt and Fear

> *When agitation and remorse are present in him, he is aware, 'Agitation and remorse are present in me.' When agitation and remorse are not present in him, he is aware, 'Agitation and remorse are not present in me.' When agitation and remorse begin to arise, he is aware of it. When already arisen agitation and remorse are abandoned, he is aware of it. When agitation and remorse already abandoned will not arise again in the future, he is aware of it.*

In Buddhist psychology, remorse or regret (Sanskrit: *kaukrtya*) is a mind function that can be either beneficial or damaging. When it's utilized to recognize errors we've made and to resolve not to commit the same mistakes in the future, then regret is a wholesome mental formation. If regret creates a guilt-complex that follows and haunts us, then it's an obstacle to our practice.

We have all made mistakes in the past. But these mistakes can be erased. We may think that because the past is gone, we can't return to the past to correct our mistakes. But the past has created the present, and if we practice mindfulness in the present, we naturally are in contact with the past. As we transform the present, we also transform the past. Our ancestors, parents, brothers, and sisters are all closely linked to us—our suffering and happiness is closely linked to theirs, just as their suffering and happiness is closely linked to ours. If we can transform ourselves, we also transform them. Our own emancipation, peace, and joy is the emancipation, peace, and joy of our ancestors and our parents. To take hold of the present in order to transform it is the unique way to bring peace, joy, and emancipation to those we love and to heal the damage done in the past.

Confession in Buddhism is based on the fact that we commit errors by means of our mind, and so by means of our mind those errors can be erased. If we take hold of life in the present moment in order to transform ourselves, we can create joy for ourselves and for everyone else as well. This transformation will bring about real joy and peace in the present and also in the future. It's not just a hollow promise to do better. If we can take hold of our breathing and live in a mindful way, thus bringing joy and happiness to ourselves and others in the present moment, we can overcome our complexes of guilt so that we're no longer paralyzed by them.

For example, the guilt complex that follows someone who has caused the death of a child out of mindlessness is a very strong complex. But if that person practices mindfulness and is able to be in real contact with the present moment, knowing what to do and what not to do in the present moment, she can save the lives of many children. Many small children die for want of medicine. Many children die through accidents or for want of proper care and attention. So she can work to save the children who are dying instead of imprisoning herself and dying slowly in the chains of regret.

Fear is also a dominant internal formation in many of us. The ground of fear is ignorance, the failure to understand our "not-self" nature. Insecurity and fear of what might happen to us and those dear to us are feelings we all have, but for some, these insecurities and fears dominate their consciousness. In Mahayana Buddhism, the bodhisattva Avalokitesvara is described as the one who has transcended all fear. He offers all beings the gift of non-fear (Sanskrit: *abhaya*), which comes from the mindful observation of the no-birth, no-death, no-increase, and no-decrease nature of all that is. The Prajñaparamita Heart Sutra is an exhortation on fearlessness. If we can observe deeply the interdependent and selfless nature of all things, we can see that there is no birth and no death and pass beyond all fear.[4]

Since everything is impermanent, disease and accidents can happen to us or to those we love at any time. We must accept this reality. If we live every moment of our lives mindfully and relate beautifully with those around us, we'll have nothing to fear and nothing to regret, even when there is a crisis in our lives. If we know that birth and death are both necessary aspects of life, we'll see that if our mother the Earth has brought us to life once, she will bring us to life one hundred thousand times more, and we will not be afraid or suffer when she reaches out her arms to welcome us back. An Awakened One remains unperturbed while riding the waves of birth and death.

Some people, because they received so many internal formations during childhood, are obsessed by feelings of insecurity. Their parents may have terrorized them, filled them with guilt, and exploited them. For people like this, receiving

---

[4] See Thich Nhat Hanh, The Heart of Understanding (Berkeley, CA: Parallax Press, 1988) for a more complete explanation of this point.

and practicing the Five Mindfulness Trainings is a most effective means of protection. Practicing the mindfulness trainings, they will be able to reestablish the balance between themselves and their environment. Taking and observing the trainings is an effective means for healing the wounds of the past and influencing society for the better in the present and the future. Practicing mindfulness in order to guard the six senses, dwell in the present moment, and be in contact with life is a wonderful way of establishing a sense of security in everyday life. If in addition we have friends who also observe and practice mindfulness, our practice will have a firm and stable support.

Exercise 20: Sowing Seeds of Peace

When the factor of awakening, joy (ease, letting go), is present in him, he is aware, 'Joy is present in me.' When joy is not present in him, he is aware, 'Joy is not present in me.' He is aware when not-yet-born joy is being born and when already-born joy is perfectly developed.

The purpose of this exercise is to sow and water the seeds of peace, joy, and liberation in us. If internal formations are the seeds of suffering, then joy, peace, and liberation are the seeds of happiness.

Buddhist psychology talks of seeds as the basis of every state of mind and the content of our consciousness. Certain seeds were transmitted to us by our parents and our ancestors. These are seeds of Buddha, Bodhisattva, Pratyekabuddha (one who has reached liberation by one's own efforts but just for one's own sake), Sravaka (one who practices as a disciple by listening to the teachings), God, Human, Warrior-God, Animal, Hungry Ghost, and Hell-Being. This means that before we were born, there were already many kinds of wholesome and unwholesome seeds in us. In addition, there are many kinds of seeds that form in us from an early age, planted by our family, school, and society. Seeds that produce suffering we can call "unwholesome," and seeds that produce happiness we can call "wholesome."

According to the principle of interdependent origination, seeds do not have a fixed nature. Every seed is dependent on every other seed for its existence, and in any one seed, all the other seeds are present. Any unwholesome seed contains within it the germ of wholesome seeds, and a wholesome seed contains within it the germ of unwholesome seeds. Just as there has to be night for there to be day and death for there to be birth, an unwholesome seed can be transformed into a wholesome seed, and a wholesome seed can be transformed into an unwholesome seed. This fact tells us that in the darkest times of our lives, in the times of the greatest suffering, the seeds of peace, joy, and happiness are still present in us. If we know how to contact the seeds of joy, peace, and happiness that are already present in us, and if we know how to water and look after them, they will germinate and bring us the fruits of peace, joy, and liberation.

The sutra is always reminding us of the two contrasting aspects of the mind. The state of mind that has no desire is a wholesome state of mind called "desirelessness." The state of mind that has no anger is a wholesome state of mind called "no-anger." Desirelessness, no-anger, and freedom are wholesome seeds in the mind that need to be watered and cared for.

The sutras often refer to the mind as a plot of ground in which all sorts of seeds are sown. That is why we have the Sanskrit term *cittabhumi*, "the mind as the earth." When we practice mindfulness, we should not just observe the phenomena of birth, old age, sickness, death, desire, hatred, aversion, ignorance, doubt, and wrong views. We should also take the time to observe objects of the mind that lead to health, joy, and emancipation in order to enable wholesome seeds to germinate and flower in the field of the mind. Observing Buddha, Dharma, Sangha, love, compassion, joy, letting go, mindfulness, investigation of dharmas, ease, happiness, and equanimity, is always encouraged in Buddhism. Joy (Sanskrit: *mudita*), for example, is not just the joy that arises from the joy of others, but also the feeling of well-being that arises in ourselves. Mudita is one of the Four

Unlimited Minds; love, compassion, and letting go or equanimity are the other three. The seeds of mudita are in all of us. Only when we have joy in our lives can we be happy and have the means to share our happiness with others. If we do not have joy, what can we share with others? If the seeds of our joy are buried under many layers of suffering, how can we smile and share joy with others? This exercise helps us stay in touch with the wholesome seeds in us so that they have a chance to develop.

Life is filled with suffering, but it is also filled with many wonderful things. There is spring as well as winter, light as well as darkness, health as well as sickness, gentle breezes and delightful rains as well as tempests and floods. Our eyes, ears, hearts, half-smiles, and breathing are wonderful phenomena. We only need to open our eyes and we can see the blue sky, the white clouds, the rose, the clear river, the golden fields of wheat, the shining eyes of a child. We only have to attune our ears to hear the whispering pines and the waves washing up on the shore. Everything is impermanent. Everything is in a temporary form. Nevertheless, there are many wonderful things. In us and around us, there are so many wondrous phenomena in nature that can refresh and heal us. If we can be in contact with them, we will receive their healing benefits. If peace and joy are in our hearts, we will gradually bring more peace and joy to the world.

The blue sky, the white clouds, the gentle breezes, the delightful rains, political stability, free speech, good schools for children, beautiful flowers, and good health—these are the positive ingredients of peace and happiness that exist alongside the negative ingredients such as war, sexism, social injustice, racial discrimination, economic inequality, and hunger and starvation. It is important that we be aware of these ugly, dangerous things in the world, so that we can begin to improve the situation. But if, day after day, we are only in contact with our anxieties and our anger about what is ugly and corrupt, we will lose our joy and our ability to serve others. That is why we have to be in contact with the peaceful and positive aspects in and around us and be able to enjoy them. We need to teach our children how to appreciate these wondrous and precious things. If we know how to appreciate them, we will know how to protect them. This basic practice will protect our happiness and our children's happiness as well.

There are many people who, although they know in theory that a flower is a wonderful thing, are unable to be in contact with it, because the sorrow in their hearts has closed them off. In the past, they may not have allowed themselves to be in contact with the refreshing, healthy seeds in their consciousness, and as a result, they are now cut off from them. The seventh precept of the Order of Interbeing reminds us to practice conscious breathing in order to stay in contact with the many healing and refreshing elements which are already around us. At times we may need the support of a friend to help us get back in touch with what is wonderful in life. "A meal needs soup as the practice needs friends" is a Vietnamese proverb about the importance of practicing with friends. Such a community of friends and fellow practitioners is called a Sangha. On the path of practice we need the support of this community, and so we say, "I take refuge in the Sangha."

Having one calm, joyful friend who is balanced and can understand and support us in times of difficulty is a great fortune. When we feel helpless, depressed, and discouraged, we can go to that friend, and, sitting with him, we can reestablish our equilibrium and once again be able to contact the flower and the other wonderful, refreshing things that exist within us and around us. If we receive the benefits of the joy that our friend brings us, we can refresh the seeds of healing in us that have become weak because they have not been cared for or watered for a long time.

The seeds of understanding, love, peace, joy, and liberation need to be sown and watered constantly by living our daily lives in mindfulness. The Sutra on the Four Establishments of Mindfulness offers many exercises for living in mindfulness. By the process of conscious breathing, smiling, walking meditation, sitting meditation, by our way of looking, listening and mindfully observing, we help the seeds of happiness flourish. The realms of love, compassion, joy, and letting go are the realms of true joy and happiness. If we have joy and can let go, we can share happiness with others and reduce their sorrows and anxieties.

Principles for the Practice of Mindfulness

DHARMAS ARE MIND

All dharmas—physical, physiological, and psychological—are objects of mind, but that does not mean that they exist separately from the mind. All Four Establishments of Mindfulness—body, feelings, mind, and dharmas—are objects of mind. Since mind and objects of mind are one, in observing its objects, mind is essentially observing mind. The word dharma in Buddhism is understood to mean the object of the mind and the content of the mind. Dharmas are classified as one of the Twelve Realms (Sanskrit: *ayatana*). The first six of these realms are the sense organs: eyes, ears, nose, tongue, body, and mind. The remaining six are form, sound, smell, taste, touch, and dharmas. Dharmas are the object of the mind, as sounds are the object of the ears. The object of cognition and the subject of cognition do not exist independently of each other. Everything that exists has to arise in the mind. The culminating phase of the development of this principle is expressed in the phrase, "All is just mind. All phenomena are just consciousness," which means, "Because of mind, all can exist. Because of consciousness, all phenomena can exist." This is developed in the Vijñaptimatra school of Mahayana Buddhism.

In the Southern traditions of Buddhism, the idea of mind as the source of all dharmas is also very clear. The term *cittasamutthana* (mind-arising) and the term *cittaja* (mind-born) are often used in the Pali Abhidhamma writings. In the Patthana (equivalent to the Sanskrit Mahapakarana), the phrase *cittam samutthanam ca rupanam* ("and mind is the arising point of forms") is found.

The object of our mindful observation can be our breath or our toe (physiological), a feeling or a perception (psychological), or a form (physical). Whether the phenomenon we observe is physiological, psychological, or physical, we know that it is not separate from our mind and is of one substance with our mind. Mind can be understood as individual mind and as collective mind. The Vijñanavada teachings make this very clear. We need to avoid thinking that the object we are observing is independent of our mind. We have to remember that it is manifested from our individual and collective consciousnesses. We observe the object of our mind in the way the right hand takes hold of the left hand. Your right hand is you and your left hand is also you. So the hand is taking hold of itself to become one with itself.

BE ONE WITH THE OBJECT OF OBSERVATION

The subject of observation is our mindfulness, which also emanates from the mind. Mindfulness has the function of illuminating and transforming. When our breathing, for example, is the object of our mindfulness, it becomes conscious breathing. Mindfulness shines its light on our breathing, transforms the forgetfulness in it into mindfulness, and gives it a calming and healing quality. Our body and our feelings are also illuminated and transformed under the light of mindfulness.

Mindfulness is the observing mind, but it does not stand outside of the object of observation. It goes right into the object and becomes one with it. Because the nature of the observing mind is mindfulness, the observing mind does not lose itself in the object but transforms it by illuminating it, just as the penetrating light of the sun transforms trees and plants.

If we want to see and understand, we have to penetrate and become one with the object. If we stand outside of it in order to observe it, we cannot really see and understand it. The work of observation is the work of penetrating and transforming. That is why the sutra says, "observing the body in the body, observing the feelings in the feelings, observing the mind in the mind, observing dharmas in dharmas." The description is very clear. The deeply observing mind is not merely an observer but a participant. Only when the observer is a participant can there be transformation.

In the practice called bare observation, mindfulness has already begun to influence the object of consciousness. When we call an in-breath an in-breath, the existence of our breath becomes very clear. Mindfulness has already penetrated our breathing. If we continue in our mindful observation, there will no longer be a duality between observer and observed. Mindfulness and breath are one. We and our breath are one. If our breath is calm, we are calm. Our breathing calms our body and our feelings. This is the method taught in the Sutra on the Four Establishments of Mindfulness and the Sutra on the Full Awareness of Breathing.

If our mind is consumed by a sense desire or by what we are observing, mindfulness is not present. Conscious breathing nourishes mindfulness, and mindfulness gives rise to conscious breathing. When mindfulness is present, we have nothing to fear. The object of our observation becomes vivid, and its source, origin, and true nature become evident. That is how it will be transformed. It no longer has the effect of binding us.

When the object of our mindful observation is totally clear, the mind that is observing is also fully revealed in great clarity. To see dharmas clearly is to see the mind clearly. When dharmas reveal themselves in their true nature, then the mind has the nature of the highest understanding. The subject and the object of cognition are not separate.

TRUE MIND AND DELUDED MIND ARE ONE

"True mind" and "deluded mind" are two aspects of the mind. Both arise from the mind. Deluded mind is the forgetful and dispersed mind, which arises from forgetfulness. The basis of true mind is awakened understanding, arising from mindfulness. Mindful observation brings out the light which exists in true mind, so that life can be revealed in its reality. In that light, confusion becomes understanding, wrong views become right views, mirages become reality, and deluded mind becomes true mind. Once mindful observation is born, it will penetrate the object of observation, illuminate it, and gradually reveal its true nature. The true mind arises from deluded mind. Things in their true nature and illusions are of the same basic substance. That is why practice is a matter of transforming deluded mind and not a matter of seeking for a true mind elsewhere. Just as the surface of a rough sea and that of the sea when it is calm are both manifestations of the same sea, true mind could not exist if there were no deluded mind. In the teaching on the Three Doors to

Liberation (Pali: *vimokkha-mukha*), aimlessness (Sanskrit: *apranihita*) is the foundation for realization. What is meant by aimlessness is that we do not seek after an object outside of ourselves. In Mahayana Buddhism, the teaching of nonattainment is the highest expression of the oneness of true mind and deluded mind.

If the rose is on its way to becoming garbage, then the garbage is also on its way to becoming a rose. She who observes discerningly will see the nondual character of the rose and the garbage. She will be able to see that there is garbage in the rose and that there are roses in the garbage. She will know that the rose needs the garbage for its existence, and the garbage needs the rose, because it is the rose that becomes garbage. Therefore, she will know how to accept the garbage in order to transform it into roses and will not be afraid when she sees the rose wither and turn into garbage. This is the principle of nonduality. If true mind (the rose) can be discovered in the raw material of deluded mind (the garbage), then we can also recognize true mind in the very substance of illusion, in the substance of birth and death.

To be liberated is not to run away from or abandon the Five Skandhas of form, feelings, perceptions, mental formations, and consciousness. Even if our body is full of impurities and even if the world is of the nature of illusion, it does not mean that to be liberated we need to run away from our body or from the world. The world of liberation and awakened understanding comes directly from this body and this world. Once Right Understanding is realized, we transcend the discriminations between pure and impure and illusory and real objects of perception. If the gardener is able to see that the rose comes directly from the garbage, then the practitioner on the path of meditation can see that nirvana comes directly from birth and death, and she no longer runs away from birth and death or seeks after nirvana. "The roots of affliction (Sanskrit: *klesa*) are the same as the awakened state. Nirvana and birth and death are illusory images in space." These quotations express deep insight into nonduality. The substance of this insight is equanimity or letting go (Sanskrit: *upeksa*), one of the Four Unlimited Minds.

The Buddha taught very clearly that we should not be attached to being or nonbeing. Being means the desire realm. Nonbeing means the realm of nihilism. To be liberated is to be free from both.

THE WAY OF NO-CONFLICT

The realization of nonduality naturally leads to the practice of offering joy, peace, and nonviolence. If the gardener knows how to deal with the organic garbage without conflict and discrimination, then the practitioner of meditation should also know how to deal with the Five

Aggregates without conflict or discrimination. The Five Aggregates are the basis of suffering and confusion, but they are also the basis of peace, joy, and liberation. We should not have an attitude of attachment or aversion to the Five Aggregates. It is clearly stated in the sutra that the practitioner observes, having put aside every craving and every distaste for this life (Pali: *vineyya loke abhijjha domanassam*).

Before realizing the awakened state, Siddhartha practiced austerities, repressing his body and his feelings. Methods such as these are violent in nature, and the results are only negative. After that period of practice, he changed and practiced nonviolence and no-conflict in relation to his body and his feelings.

The method taught by the Buddha in the Sutra on the Four Establishments of Mindfulness clearly expresses the spirit of nonviolence and no-conflict. Mindfulness recognizes what is happening in the body and the mind and then continues to illuminate and observe the object deeply. During this practice, there is no craving for, running after, or repressing the object. This is the true meaning of the term bare observation. There is no coveting and no distaste. We know that our body and our feelings are ourselves and therefore we do not repress them, because to do so would be to repress ourselves. On the contrary, we accept our body and our feelings. Accepting does not mean craving. By accepting, we naturally reach a degree of peace and understanding. Peace and joy arise when we drop the discrimination between right and wrong; between the mind that observes and the body that is being observed (which we say is impure); between the mind that observes and the feelings that are being observed (which we say are painful).

When we accept our body and our feelings, we treat them in an affectionate, nonviolent way. The Buddha taught us to practice mindfulness of physiological and psychological phenomena in order to observe them, not in order to suppress them. When we accept our body, make peace with it, and calm its functioning, not feeling aversion to it, we are following the teachings of the Buddha: "Breathing in, I am aware of my whole body. Breathing out, I am calming the functions of my body." (Sutra on the Full Awareness of Breathing). In observation meditation, we do not turn ourselves into a battlefield with the good side fighting the bad. When we can see the nonduality of the rose and the garbage, the roots of affliction and the awakened mind, we are no longer afraid. We accept our afflictions, look after them as a mother looks after her child, and transform them.

When we recognize the roots of affliction in us and become one with them, whether we are entrapped in them or not depends on our state of mind. When we are forgetful, we may be caught by our roots of affliction, and so we become our roots of affliction. When we are mindful, we can see our roots of affliction clearly and transform them. Therefore, it is essential to see our roots of affliction in mindfulness. As long as the lamp of mindfulness shines its light, the darkness is transformed. We need to nourish mindfulness in ourselves by the practices of conscious breathing, hearing the sound of a bell, reciting gathas, and many other skillful means.

We need an attitude of kindness and nonviolence toward our body. We should not look on our body as only an instrument or mistreat it. When we are tired or in pain, our body is trying to tell us that it is not happy and at ease. The body has its own language. As practitioners of mindfulness, we should know what our body is saying to us. When we feel a lot of pain in our legs during sitting meditation, we should smile and change our position slowly and gently in mindfulness. There is nothing wrong with changing our position. It does not waste our time. As long as mindfulness is maintained, the work of meditation continues. We should not bully ourselves. When we push ourselves around like that, not only do we lose our peace of mind and our joy, but we also lose our mindfulness and concentration. We practice sitting meditation to have liberation, peace, and joy, not to become a hero who is capable of enduring a lot of pain.

We also need a nonviolent attitude with regard to our feelings. Because we know that our feelings are ourselves, we do not neglect or overrule them. We embrace them affectionately in the arms of mindfulness, as a mother embraces her newborn child when it cries. A mother embraces the child with all her love for the child to feel comforted and stop crying. Mindfulness nourished by conscious breathing takes the feelings in its arms, becomes one with them, calms and transforms them.

Before the Buddha attained full realization of the path, he tried various methods of using the mind to suppress the mind, and he failed. That is why he chose to practice in a nonviolent way. The Buddha recounted in the Mahasaccaka Sutra (Madhyama Agama 36):

> I thought, why do I not grit my teeth, press my tongue against my palate, use my mind to overrule my mind, use my mind to repress my mind? Then, as a wrestler might take hold of the head or the shoulders of someone weaker than him, and, in order to restrain and coerce that person, he has to hold him down constantly without letting go for a moment, so I gritted my teeth, pressed my tongue against my palate, and used my mind to overrule and suppress my mind. As I did this, I was bathed in sweat. Although I was not lacking in strength, although I maintained mindfulness and did not fall from mindfulness, my body and my mind were not at peace, and I was worn out by these exhausting efforts. This practice caused other feelings of pain to arise in me

besides the pain associated with the austerities, and I was not able to tame my mind.

It is clear from this passage that the Buddha regarded this kind of practice as not useful. Yet, this passage was inserted into the Vitakkasanthana Sutra (Majjhima Nikaya 20), with the opposite meaning to what the Buddha intended:

Just as a wrestler takes hold of the head or the shoulders of someone weaker than himself, restrains and coerces that person, and holds him down constantly, not letting go one moment, so a monk who meditates in order to stop all unwholesome thoughts of desire and aversion, when these thoughts continue to arise, should grit his teeth, press his tongue against his palate, and do his best to use his mind to beat down and defeat his mind.

This same passage was inserted into the Sutra on the Four Grounds of Mindfulness which appears as the second version in this book (see Appendix): "The practitioner who observes body as body closes his lips tightly or grits his teeth, presses his tongue against his palate, and uses his mind to restrain and to oppose his mind." This extract does not appear in most versions of the sutra (see the first and third versions), but is also found in the Kayasmrti Sutra (Madhyama Agama 81) whose content is very similar to that of our second version. The corresponding sutra in Pali is the Kayagatasati Sutta (Majjhima Nikaya 119).

OBSERVATION IS NOT INDOCTRINATION

In Buddhist practice centers throughout the world, students are taught to recite such phrases as "body is impure, feelings are suffering, mind is impermanent, dharmas are without self," as they observe the Four Establishments. I was taught in this way as a novice, and I always felt that it was a kind of brainwashing.

The method of the Four Establishments of Mindfulness is observing deeply in the spirit of "not craving and not feeling distaste." Mindfulness does not cling, push away, reprimand, or repress, so that the true nature of all dharmas can reveal itself in the light of mindful observation. That the impermanent, selfless, and impure nature of all dharmas has the effect of causing suffering can be seen while we observe dharmas, but that is not because we repeat some formulas like the above, in an automatic way. When we look deeply and see the true nature of all dharmas, they will reveal themselves.

When we mechanically repeat, "Body is impure," we are reciting a dogma. If we observe all physiological phenomena and see their impure nature, this is not dogma. It is our experience. If, during our mindful observation, we see that phenomena are sometimes pure and sometimes impure, then that is our experience. If we look even more deeply and see that phenomena are neither pure nor impure, that they transcend the concepts of pure and impure, we discover what is taught in the Heart of the Prajñaparamita Sutra. This sutra also teaches us to resist all dogmatic attitudes. We should not force ourselves to see the body as impure or the feelings as suffering. Although there may be some truth in the sentences, just repeating them dogmatically has the effect of cramming us with knowledge. While we observe in mindfulness, we may see that we have many painful feelings, but we will also see that we have many joyful and peaceful feelings and many neutral feelings. And if we look more deeply, we will see that neutral feelings can become joyful feelings, and that suffering and happiness are interdependent. Suffering is, because happiness is; and happiness is, because suffering is. When we repeat, "Mind is impermanent," our attitude is still dogmatic. If the mind is impermanent, then the body must be impermanent and the feelings too. The same is true of "Dharmas are selfless." If dharmas are selfless, so are body, mind, and feelings.

Therefore, the special teaching of the Sutra on the Four Establishments of Mindfulness is to observe all dharmas but not to have any fixed ideas, just to keep on observing mindfully without comment, without assuming any attitude towards the object you are observing. In this way, the true nature of the object will be able to reveal itself in the light of mindful observation, and you will have insight into wonderful discoveries such as no-birth no-death, neither pure nor impure, neither increasing nor decreasing, interpenetration, and interbeing.

Conclusion

The last part of the Sutra on the Four Establishments of Mindfulness reads: "He who practices the Four Establishments of Mindfulness for seven years can expect one of two fruits: the highest understanding in this very life or, if there remains some residue of affliction, he can attain the fruit of no-return. Let alone seven years, bhikkhus, whoever practices the Four Establishments of Mindfulness for six, five, four, three, two years, or one year, or even six, five, four, three, two months, one month or half a month can also expect one of two fruits: either the highest understanding or the fruit of no-return. It may take seven years to attain the fruits of the practice, but people who have great willingness to practice don't need seven years; it is enough to have half a month. That is why we say that this path of the Establishments of Mindfulness is the most wonderful path, which helps beings realize purification, transcend grief and sorrow, and destroy pain and anxiety. The bhikkhus were delighted to hear the teaching of the Buddha. They took it to heart and began to put it into practice."

Mindfulness is the core of Buddhist practice. This practice can be done not only in sitting meditation but also in every minute of our daily life. When we are able to take hold of our body in mindfulness, we begin to master our mind, and our body and mind become one. If our practice of mindfulness is still weak, our body is like a wild buffalo. Mindfulness is the herdsman and our mind is the wild buffalo.

The Ten Oxherding Paintings of the Zen tradition represent stages on the path of awakening, stages on the path of mastering the body and mind. In the beginning the trainer approaches the wild buffalo; trainer and buffalo are two separate entities. With the practice of mindfulness, the trainer comes to know the buffalo. Gradually, the trainer and the buffalo become one, and eventually the trainer is able to ride on the back of the buffalo, singing or playing the flute, and the buffalo can go wherever he likes.

When we stand, walk, sit, lie down, or work in mindfulness, we are practicing what the Buddha taught us in the sutra. But in order for the practice to be easy and successful, it is very helpful to practice with a community, called a Sangha. The presence of those who practice mindful living is a great support and encouragement to us. Seeing people walking, sitting, being, and doing things in mindfulness, we are reminded to maintain mindfulness ourselves. In Buddhist communities, people use bells of mindfulness to remind one another to practice. The bell sounds from time to time and calls us back to being mindful. The presence of the people who practice around us is equivalent to the presence of several bells of mindfulness.

With a Sangha, we get support whenever we need it, and we profit from the experience and insight of its members and also from their advice and guidance. A teacher is a treasure, but without a Sangha, the practice can still be difficult.

Therefore getting in touch with an existing Sangha or setting up a small Sangha around us is a very important step. We should be able to participate from time to time in a retreat of five days or a week to practice mindfulness in a concentrated atmosphere. With friends we can organize from time to time a Day of Mindfulness to practice together. A Day of Mindfulness can also be organized in the family for all the adults and children to practice together. It is good if we can invite a number of friends to join us.

Practicing Buddhist meditation is not a way of avoiding society or family life. The correct practice of mindfulness can help us bring peace, joy, and release both to ourselves and to our family and friends as well. Those who practice mindful living will inevitably transform themselves and their way of life. They will live a more simple life and will have more time to enjoy themselves, their friends, and their natural environment. They will have more time to offer joy to others and to alleviate their suffering. And when the time comes, they will die in peace. They will know that to die is to begin anew or just to continue with another form of life. When we live our life this way, every day is a Happy Birthday, a Happy Continuation Day.

Appendix

Three Versions of the Sutra

A NOTE ON THE HISTORY OF THE TEXTS

During his lifetime, the Buddha delivered his discourses in the Ardhamagadhi language. But his teachings spread far beyond the area where that language was spoken, and there is no doubt that in the practice centers that lay beyond the alluvial plain of the Ganges River, the monks and nuns would have studied the Dharma in their own local languages. One day in the Jetavana monastery, two monks, Yamelu and Tekula, asked the Buddha if they could translate all his teachings into the classical meter of the Vedic language. They told the Buddha that they wanted to do so in order to protect the beauty and accuracy of the Dharma. But the Buddha did not want his teachings to become a precious object reserved for a scholarly elite. He wanted everyone to be able to study and practice the Dharma in her own language.

About four months after the passing of the Buddha, the Venerable Mahakasyapa convened a council on Mount Saptaparnaguha at Rajgir in order to orally collate the Sutra and Vinaya

Pitakas. Five hundred elder bhikkhus were invited to attend this Collation Council, which was sponsored by King Ajatasatru of Magadha. The language of the collation would naturally have been Ardhamagadhi, the language of the Buddha. If the local districts later developed versions in their own languages, these would have been based on the collation of the Rajgir Council.

One hundred years later, a second council was convened in Vaisali to further collate the canon of the Buddha's teachings. On this occasion, seven hundred bhikkhus were invited to attend. After the Second Council, in 375BCE, the community of bhikkhus divided itself into two schools: the Sthavira, which tended to be conservative, and the Mahasanghika, which tended to promote development and reform. The followers of the Mahasanghika were more numerous. In the three hundred years that followed, many other schools branched off from these two schools. According to the Samayabhedoparacanacakra by Vasumitra, who belonged to the Sarvastivada school of the Northern tradition, there were eighteen schools in all.

The number of schools proliferated because of the many different ways of understanding and commenting on the teachings of the Buddha. The works in which these explanations are contained are called the Abhidharma and belong to the Sastra Pitaka. Each school has handed down its own versions of the Vinaya, Sutra, and Sastra

Pitakas. All three pitakas of the Theravada school are intact thanks to the relatively stable ground for practice in Sri Lanka. The Tripitaka of this school is written in the Pali language, which originated in western India. The Theravada arose from the Vibhajyavada, which was a school opposing the Sarvastivada.

A third council was organized at Pataliputra under the patronage of King Asoka in 244BCE, two hundred thirty-six years after the passing of the Buddha. At that time, perhaps because King Asoka leaned more towards the Vibhajyavada sect, the Sarvastivadins moved to the north and established their base for development in Kashmir, where they flourished for more than one thousand years.

Three versions of the Sutra on the Four Establishments of Mindfulness have come down to us. The main version presented in this book is a translation from the Pali Satipatthana Sutta (number 10 in the Majjhima Nikaya), a first century BCE scripture of the Theravada School. This version is exactly the same as the Pali Mahasatipatthana Sutta (number 20 in the Digha Nikaya), except that the latter has a little more text at the end. For purposes of this commentary, the Mahasatipatthana Sutta is regarded as version one.

The second and third versions are from the Chinese Canon. The second version, the Sutra on the Four Grounds of Mindfulness, is a translation of the Nian Chu Jing (number 98 in the Madhyama Agama and number 26 in the Taisho Revised Tripitaka) of the Sarvastivada school, translated into Chinese from the Sanskrit Smrtyupasthana Sutra. The third version, The One Way In Sutra, is a translation of the Yi Ru Dao Jing (Ekottara Agama, sutra number 125 in the Taisho Revised Tripitaka). It comes from the Mahasanghika school, not in its original but in its later form.

In the Chinese Canon, the name of the translator of the Sutra on the Four Grounds of Mindfulness is given as Gautama Sanghadeva. Master Sanghadeva came from what is now Afghanistan and traveled to China in the fourth century, living from the year 383 in the capital Chang An, and after that in Jian Kang, the capital of Dong Chin. He began the work of translation between 391 and 398. He probably had learned Chinese when he lived in Chang An.

The Chinese Canon also ascribes the translation of The One Way In Sutra to Gautama Sanghadeva. However, there are many reasons for thinking that the sutra was translated by the monk Dharmanandi. Master Dharmanandi was Khotanese. He traveled to China in the fourth century and took up residence in Chang An, where he translated sutras from 384–391. The book *Marking the Era of Buddhism* (K'ai Yuan Shi Pi Chiao Lu) says that the Ekottara Agama was translated by Sanghadeva. Master Tao An, in his introduction to The One Way In Sutra, says that it was Master Dharmanandi who read the original

Sanskrit version for Zhu Fo Nian to translate into Chinese and for Gautama Sanghadeva to write down. After that, they brought the translated version to be examined by the translation school of Master Sanghadeva in Jian Kang, the capital of Dong Chin.

The Li Tai San Pao Chi, Volume 7 (Sui Dynasty), the Ta T'ang Nei Tien Lu, and the Ta T'ang Ch'an Ting Chung Ching Mu Lu, all say that there were two translations of the Ekottara Agama, one by Master Dharmanandi and one by Master Sanghadeva. The books Ch'u San Tsang Chi Chi and the Chung Ching Mu Lu of the Sui Dynasty, and the Sutra Index of the T'ang Dynasty, all say that the Ekottara Agama was translated by Master Dharmanandi. Judging from all of this information and from the literary style of the text, we conclude that there was only one translation of the Ekottara Agama, the translation of Master Dharmanandi.

The Mahasanghika school, which came into existence after the council at Vaisali, later divided into two branches, one going to the northwest and one to the south. There were five branches of Mahasanghika in the northwest, including the Lokottaravada, which was Mahayana in outlook. It was the Ekottara Agama of this branch, including the third version of the sutra on mindfulness presented in this book, that Dharmanandi translated. Therefore, our third version is more influenced by the Mahayana and can be said to be less close to the original teaching of the Buddha than the first two versions, because many later elements have infiltrated into it. Still, it contains the essence of the original teachings.

VERSION TWO: SUTRA ON THE FOUR GROUNDS OF MINDFULNESS

Nian Chu Jing (Sarvastivada) from Madhya Agama (number 26 in Taisho Revised Tripitaka). Translated by Gautama Sanghadeva from Sanskrit into Chinese, and by Thich Nhat Hanh and Annabel Laity into English.

I.

I heard these words of the Buddha one time when the Lord was staying in the town of Kammassadharma in the land of the Kuru people.

The Lord addressed the bhikkhus:

"There is a path which can help beings realize purification, overcome anxiety and fear, end pain, distress, and grief, and attain the right practice. This is the path of dwelling in the Four Grounds of Mindfulness. All the Tathagatas of the past have attained the fruit of true awakening, the state of no further obstacles, by establishing their minds in the Four Grounds of Mindfulness. Relying on these Four Grounds, they have abandoned the Five Hindrances, purged the poisons of the mind, been able to transcend the circumstances which obstruct awakened understanding, and, practicing according to the Seven Factors of Awakening, have attained the true, right, and highest awakening. All Tathagatas of the future will also attain the fruit of true awakening, the state of no more obstacles, thanks to establishing their minds in the Four Grounds of Mindfulness. Relying on the Four Grounds of Mindfulness, they will be able to put an end to the Five Hindrances, purge the poisons of the mind, and overcome whatever weakens the ability to understand, practice the Seven Factors of Awakening, and attain the true, right, and highest awakening. All Tathagatas of the present (including myself) have attained the fruit of true awakening, the state without obstacles, thanks to establishing their minds in the Four Grounds of Mindfulness. Relying on the Four Grounds of Mindfulness, we have been able to put an end to the Five Hindrances and overcome whatever weakens the ability to understand, practice the Seven Factors of Awakening and attain to the true, right, and highest awakening.

"What are the Four Grounds of Mindfulness? They are the four methods of observing body as body, feelings as feelings, mind as mind, and objects of mind as objects of mind."

II.

"What is the way to remain established in the awareness of body as body?

"When the practitioner walks, he knows he is walking. When he stands, he knows he is standing. When he sits, he knows he is sitting. When he lies down, he knows he is lying down. When he wakes up, he knows he is waking up. Awake or asleep, he knows he is awake or asleep. This is how the practitioner is aware of body as body, both inside the body and outside the body, and establishes mindfulness in the body with understanding, insight, clarity, and realization. This is called being aware of body as body.

"Further, bhikkhus, when practicing awareness of the body, the practitioner is clearly aware of the positions and movements of the body, such as going out and coming in, bending down and standing up, extending limbs, or drawing them in. When wearing the sanghati robe, carrying the alms bowl, walking, standing, lying, sitting, speaking, or being silent, he knows the skillful way of being aware. This is how the practitioner is aware of body as body, from both within and from without, and establishes mindfulness in the body with understanding, insight, clarity, and realization. This is called being aware of body as body.

"Further, bhikkhus, a practitioner is aware of body as body so that whenever an unwholesome state of mind arises, he can immediately apply a wholesome state to counterbalance and transform the unwholesome state of mind. Just as a carpenter or carpenter's apprentice stretches out a piece of string along the edge of a plank of wood and with a plane trims off the edge of the plank, so the practitioner, when he feels an unwholesome state of mind arising, immediately uses a wholesome state of mind to counterbalance and transform the existing state. This is how the practitioner is aware of body as body, from both within and from without, and establishes mindfulness in the body with understanding, insight, clarity, and realization. This is called being aware of body as body.

"Further, bhikkhus, a practitioner is aware of body as body when, closing his lips tight, clenching his teeth, pressing his tongue against his palate, taking one part of his mind to restrain another part of his mind, he counterbalances a thought and transforms it. Just as two strong men might hold onto a weak man and easily restrain him, so the practitioner presses his lips together and clenches his teeth, presses his tongue against his palate, takes one part of his mind to restrain another part of his mind, to counterbalance and transform a thought. This is how the practitioner is aware of body as body, from both within and from without, and establishes mindfulness in the body with understanding, insight, clarity, and realization. This is called being aware of body as body.

"Further, bhikkhus, a practitioner is aware of body as body, when, breathing in, he knows that he is breathing in, and breathing out, he knows that he is breathing out. When breathing in a long breath, he knows that he is breathing in a long breath. When breathing out a long breath, he knows that he is breathing out a long breath. When breathing in, he is aware of his whole body. Breathing out, he is aware of his whole body. Breathing in and out, he is aware of what he is doing and he practices stopping while acting. Breathing in and out, he is aware of what he is saying and he practices stopping while speaking. This is how the practitioner is aware of body as body, from both within and from without, and establishes mindfulness in the body, with recognition, insight, clarity, and realization. This is called being aware of body as body.

"Further, bhikkhus, a practitioner is aware of body as body, when, thanks to having put aside the Five Desires, a feeling of bliss arises during his concentration and saturates every part of his body. This feeling of bliss which arises during concentration reaches every part of his body. Like the bath attendant who, after putting powdered soap into a basin, mixes it with water until the soap paste has water in every part of it, so the practitioner feels the bliss which is born when the desires of the sense realms are put aside, saturate every part of his body. This is how the practitioner is aware of body as body, from both within and from without, and establishes mindfulness in the body with recognition, insight, clarity, and realization. This is called being aware of body as body.

"Further, bhikkhus, a practitioner who is aware of body as body, feels the joy which arises during concentration saturate every part of his body. There is no part of his body this feeling of joy, born during concentration, does not reach. Like a spring within a mountain whose clear water flows out and down all sides of that mountain and bubbles up in places where water has not previously entered, saturating the entire mountain, in the same way, joy, born during concentration, permeates the whole of the practitioner's body; it is present everywhere. This is how the practitioner is aware of body as body, from both within and from without, and establishes mindfulness in the body with recognition, insight, clarity, and realization. This is called being aware of body as body.

"Further, bhikkhus, a practitioner who is aware of body as body, experiences a feeling of happiness which arises with the disappearance of the feeling of joy and permeates his whole body. This feeling of happiness which arises with the disappearance of the feeling of joy reaches every part of his body. Just as the different species of blue, pink, red, and white lotus which grow up from the bottom of a pond of clear water and appear on the surface of that pond have their tap roots, subsidiary roots, leaves, and flowers all full of the water of that pond, and there is no part of the plant which does not contain the water, so the feeling of happiness which arises with the disappearance of joy permeates the whole of the practitioner's body, and there is no part which it does not penetrate. This is how the practitioner is aware of body as body, from both within and from without, and establishes mindfulness in the body with recognition, insight, clarity, and realization, and that is called being aware of body as body.

"Further, bhikkhus, a practitioner who is aware of body as body, envelops the whole of his body with a clear, calm mind, filled with understanding. Just as someone who puts on a very long robe which reaches from his head to his feet, and there is no part of his body which is not covered by this robe, so the practitioner with a clear, calm mind envelops his whole body in understanding and leaves no part of the body untouched. This is how the practitioner is aware of body as body, from both within and from without, and establishes mindfulness in the body with recognition, insight, clarity, and realization. This is called being aware of body as body.

"Further, bhikkhus, a practitioner who is aware of body as body, is aware of clear light, knows how to welcome clear light, practice with and recall to mind clear light, whether it comes from in front to behind him or from behind to in front of him, day and night, above and below him, with a mind which is well-balanced and not hindered. He practices "the one way in" by means of clear light, and finally his mind is not obscured in darkness. This is how the practitioner is aware of body as body, from both within and from without, and establishes mindfulness in the body with recognition, insight, clarity, and realization. This is called being aware of body as body.

"Further, bhikkhus, a practitioner who is aware of body as body, knows how to use the meditational 'sign' skillfully and knows how to maintain the object of meditation skillfully. As someone sitting observes someone lying down and someone lying down observes someone sitting, so the practitioner knows how to recognize the meditational sign and use it skillfully and knows how skillfully to maintain the object of meditation. This is how the practitioner is aware of body as body, from both within and from without, and establishes mindfulness in the body with recognition, insight, clarity, and realization. This is called being aware of body as body.

"Further, bhikkhus, a practitioner who is aware of the body, knows very well that this body exists due to the interdependence of the parts of the body, from the top of the head to the soles of the feet. He sees that all the parts of the body are impure. In his body are the hairs of the head, the hairs of the body, the fingernails, teeth, hard skin, soft skin, flesh, sinews, bones, heart, kidneys, liver, lungs, large intestine, small intestine, gallbladder, stomach, excrement, brain, tears, sweat, sputum, saliva, pus, blood, grease, marrow, bladder, urine. He sees all these clearly as someone with good eyesight sees in a cask full of all sorts of grains that this is rice, this is millet, this is mustard seed, and so on. The practitioner who takes his attention throughout his body knows that it only exists in dependence on the true value of the parts out of which it is made, from the top of the head to the soles of the feet, and sees that all those parts are impure. This is how the practitioner is aware of body as body, from both within and from without, and establishes mindfulness in the body with recognition, insight, clarity, and realization. This is called being aware of body as body.

"Further, bhikkhus, a practitioner who is aware of body as body, observes the elements which comprise his body: 'In this very body of mine, there is the element earth, the element water, the element fire, the element air, the element space, and the element consciousness.' Just as a butcher, after killing the cow and skinning it, lays out the meat on the ground in six parts, so the practitioner observes the six elements of which the body is comprised: 'Here is the earth element in my body, here is the water element, here is the fire element, here is the air element, here is the space element, and here is the consciousness element.' This is how the practitioner is aware of body as body, from both within and from without, and establishes mindfulness in the body with understanding, insight, clarity, and realization. This is called being aware of body as body.

"Further, bhikkhus, a practitioner who is meditating on body as body visualizes a corpse. It is one to seven days old and has been disemboweled by vultures and torn by wolves. It is either distended or rotting, having been thrown onto the charnel ground or buried in the earth. When the practitioner visualizes a corpse like this, he compares it with his own body: 'This body of mine will also undergo a state such as this. In the end, there is no way it can avoid this condition.' This is how the practitioner is aware of body as body, from both within and from without, and establishes mindfulness in the body with recognition, insight, clarity, and realization. This is called being aware of body as body.

"Further, bhikkhus, a practitioner who meditates on body as body visualizes a bluish corpse, decayed and half-gnawed away, lying in a heap on the ground. When the practitioner visualizes a corpse like this, he compares it with his own body: 'This body of mine will also undergo a state such as this. In the end, there is no way it can avoid this condition.' This is how the practitioner is aware of body as body, from both within and from without, and establishes mindfulness in the body with recognition, insight, clarity, and realization. This is called being aware of body as body.

"Further, bhikkhus, a practitioner who meditates on body as body visualizes a skeleton which has no skin, flesh, blood, or bloodstains. There are only the bones held together by sinews. When the practitioner visualizes a skeleton like this, he compares it with his own body: 'This body of mine will also undergo a state such as this. In the end, there is no way it can avoid this condition.' This is how the practitioner is aware of body as body, from both within and from without, and establishes mindfulness in the body with recognition, insight, clarity, and realization. This is called being aware of body as body.

"Further, bhikkhus, a practitioner who meditates on body as body visualizes the bones scattered in different directions: foot bone, shin bone, thigh bone, clavicle, spinal column, shoulder blade, tarsus, skull—each one in a different place. When he visualizes them like this, he compares it with his own body: 'This body of mine will also undergo a state such as this. In the end, there is no way it can avoid this condition.' This is how the practitioner is aware of body as body, from both within and from without, and establishes mindfulness in the body with understanding, insight, clarity, and realization. This is called being aware of body as body.

"Further, bhikkhus, a practitioner who meditates on body as body, visualizes the bones bleached to the color of shells or the color of a dove, and the bones which have rotted down to form a powder. When he visualizes them like this, he compares it with his own body: 'This body of mine will also undergo a state such as this. In the end, there is no way it can avoid this condition.' This is how the practitioner is aware of body as body, from both within and from without, and establishes mindfulness in the body with recognition, insight, clarity, and realization. This is called being aware of body as body."

III.

"What is the way to remain established in the meditation on feelings as feelings?

"When the practitioner has a pleasant feeling, he knows immediately that he has a pleasant feeling. When he has an unpleasant feeling, he knows immediately that he has an unpleasant feeling. When he has a neutral feeling, he knows immediately that he has a neutral feeling. When there is a pleasant feeling, an unpleasant feeling, or a neutral feeling in the body; a pleasant feeling, an unpleasant feeling, or a neutral feeling in the mind; a pleasant feeling, an unpleasant feeling, or a neutral feeling of this world; a pleasant feeling, an unpleasant feeling, or a neutral feeling not of this world; a pleasant feeling, an unpleasant feeling, or a neutral feeling associated with desire; a pleasant feeling, an unpleasant feeling, or a neutral feeling not associated with desire, he is clearly aware of this. This is how the practitioner is aware of feelings as feelings, from both within and from without, and establishes right mindfulness. If there are bhikkhus and bhikkhunis who meditate on feelings as feelings, according to these instructions, then they are capable of dwelling in the meditation on feelings as feelings."

IV.

"What is the way to remain established in the meditation on mind as mind?

"When the practitioner's mind is attached to something, he knows it is attached to something. When the practitioner's mind is not attached, he knows it is not attached. When the practitioner's mind hates something, he knows that it hates something. When his mind is not hating, he knows it is not hating. When his mind is confused, he knows it is confused. When it is not confused, he knows it is not confused. When his mind is defiled, he knows it is defiled. When his mind is not defiled, he knows it is not defiled. When it is distracted, he knows it is distracted. When it is not distracted, he knows it is not distracted. When his mind has obstacles, he knows it has obstacles. When it has no obstacles, he knows it has no obstacles. When it is tense, he knows it is tense. When it is not tense, he knows it is not tense. When it is boundless, he knows it is boundless. When it is bound, he knows it is bound. When his mind is concentrating, he knows it is concentrating. When it is not concentrating, he knows it is not concentrating. When his mind is not liberated, he knows it is not liberated. When it is liberated, he knows it is liberated. That is how the practitioner is aware of mind as mind, from both within and from without, and establishes mindfulness in the mind with recognition, insight, clarity, and realization, and that is called being aware of mind as mind. If bhikkhus or bhikkhunis meditate on mind as mind according to the details of these instructions, then they know how to dwell in the practice of observing mind as mind."

V.

"What is the way to remain established in the meditation on objects of mind as objects of mind?

"When the practitioner realizes that his eyes in contact with form give rise to an internal formation, then he knows without any doubt that an internal formation is being formed. If there is no internal formation, he knows without any doubt that there is no internal formation. If an internal formation that had not arisen formerly now arises, he knows this. If an internal formation that had arisen formerly now comes to an end and will not arise again, he knows this. The same is true with all the other sense organs: ears, nose, tongue, body, and mind. When these sense organs are in contact with an external object and bring about an internal formation, then the practitioner knows without any doubt that there is an internal formation. If an internal formation which had not arisen formerly now arises, he knows this. If an internal formation which had arisen formerly now comes to an end and will not arise again, he knows this. This is how the practitioner is aware of objects of mind as objects of mind, from both within and from without, and establishes mindfulness in the object of mind with recognition, insight, clarity, and realization. This is called being aware of objects of mind as objects of mind. If bhikkhus or bhikkhunis meditate on objects of mind as objects of mind according to these instructions, then they know how to dwell in the practice of observing objects of mind as objects of mind with regard to the six realms of consciousness.

"Further, bhikkhus, when the practitioner is meditating on objects of mind as objects of mind, if he sees sensual desire in himself, he knows without any doubt that sensual desire is there. If he sees no sensual desire in himself, he knows without any doubt that no sensual desire is there. If a sensual desire that had not arisen formerly now arises, he knows this without any doubt. If a sensual desire that had arisen formerly now comes to an end, he also knows this without any doubt. The same is true of the four other obstacles: anger, torpor, agitation, and doubt. If there is doubt in his mind, he knows for certain that there is doubt. If there is no doubt in his mind, he knows for certain that there is no doubt. When a formally nonexistent doubt arises, he knows that for certain. When an already arisen doubt comes to an end, he also knows that for certain. That is how the practitioner is aware of objects of mind as objects of mind, from both within and from without, and establishes mindfulness in the object of mind with recognition, insight, clarity, and realization, and that is called being aware of objects of mind as objects of mind. If bhikkhus or bhikkhunis meditate on objects of mind as objects of mind according to the details of these instructions, then they know how to dwell in the practice of observing objects of mind as objects of mind with regard to the Five Obstacles.

"Further bhikkhus, when the practitioner is meditating on objects of mind as objects of mind, if he sees in his mind the Factor of Awakening, mindfulness, he knows without any doubt that mindfulness is there. When mindfulness is not present, he knows without a doubt that mindfulness is not present. When mindfulness which had formerly not been present is now present, the practitioner also knows this without any doubt. When mindfulness has arisen and is still present, is not lost, does not decline but actually increases, the practitioner is also aware of all this. The same is true of all the other Factors of Awakening—the investigation of dharmas, energy, joy, ease, concentration, and letting go. When letting go is present in his mind, he knows without a doubt that letting go is present. When letting go is not present, he knows without a doubt that letting go is not present. When letting go that had formerly not been present is now present, the practitioner also knows this without any doubt. When letting go has arisen and is still present, is not lost, does not decline, but actually increases, the practitioner is also aware of all this. This is how the practitioner is aware of objects of mind as objects of mind, from both within and from without, and establishes mindfulness in the object of mind with understanding, insight, clarity, and realization, and that is called being aware of objects of mind as objects of mind. If bhikkhus or bhikkhunis meditate on objects of mind as objects of mind according to these instructions, then they know how to dwell in the practice of meditating on objects of mind as objects of mind with regard to the Seven Factors of Awakening."

VI.

"Any bhikkhu or bhikkhuni who practices being established in the Four Grounds of Mindfulness for seven years will certainly realize one of two fruits—either attaining in this very life the highest understanding or the fruit of

Arhat with some residue of ignorance. And not just seven, or six, or five, or four, or three, or two years, or one year. A bhikkhu or a bhikkhuni who practices being established in the Four Grounds of Mindfulness for seven months will certainly realize one of two fruits—either attaining in this very life the highest understanding or the fruit of Arhat with some residue from former deeds. And not just seven months, or six, five, four, three, two months, or one month. A bhikkhu or a bhikkhuni who practices being established in the Four Grounds of Mindfulness for seven days and seven nights will certainly realize one of two fruits—either attaining in this very life the highest understanding or the fruit of Arhat with some residue from former deeds. Not to mention seven days and seven nights, six days and nights, five days and nights, four days and nights, three days and nights, two days and nights, or one day and night, a bhikkhu or a bhikkhuni who practices being established in the Four Grounds of Mindfulness for just a few hours, if she begins the practice in the morning, by the evening there will have been progress, and if she begins in the afternoon, by nightfall there will have been progress."

After the Lord Buddha had spoken, the bhikkhus and bhikkhunis who heard him teach were delighted to carry out the Buddha's teachings.

VERSION THREE: THE ONE WAY IN SUTRA

Yi Ru Dao Jing (Mahasanghika) from Ekottara Agama, chapter 12. Translated by Dharmanandi from Sanskrit into Chinese, and by Thich Nhat Hanh and Annabel Laity into English.

I.

I heard these words of the Buddha one time when he was staying in the Jeta Grove in the town of Sravasti. The Lord addressed the assembly of monks:

"There is a way to practice which purifies the actions of living beings, eradicates all sorrow, anxiety, and the roots of afflictions, and leads to the highest understanding and the realization of nirvana. It is a path which destroys the Five Obstacles. It is the path of the Four Ways of Stopping and Concentrating the Mind. Why is it called 'the one way in?' Because it is the way to the oneness of mind. Why is it called a way? Because it is the Noble Eightfold Path, the way of right view, right contemplation, right action, right livelihood, right practice, right speech, right mindfulness, and right concentration. This explains the expression 'the one way in.'

"What then are the Five Obstacles? They are attachment, aversion, agitation, torpor, and doubt. These are the obstacles which need to be removed.

"What are the Four Ways of Stopping and Concentrating the Mind? The practitioner meditates on the body in the body from within to end unwholesome thoughts and remove anxiety, and he meditates on the body in the body from without to end unwholesome thoughts and remove anxiety. The practitioner meditates on the feelings in the feelings from within and from without in order to be at peace and have joy, and he meditates on the feelings in the feelings from both within and from without in order to be at peace and have joy. The practitioner meditates on the mind in the mind from within, and he meditates on the mind in the mind from without in order to be at peace and have joy, and he meditates on the mind in the mind from both within and from without in order to be at peace and have joy. The practitioner meditates on the objects of mind in the objects of mind from within, and he meditates on the objects of mind in the objects of mind from without in order to be at peace and have joy, and he meditates on the objects of mind in the objects of mind from both within and from without in order to be at peace and have joy."

II.

"How does the practitioner meditate on the body from within so as to realize peace and joy in himself?

"In this case, the practitioner meditates on the nature and functions of the body. When he examines it from head to toes or from toes to head, he sees that it is composed of impure constituents, and he is unable to be attached to it. He observes that this body has hair of the head and hair of the body, nails, teeth, skin, flesh, sinews, bones, marrow, sweat, pus, stomach, small intestine, large intestine, heart, liver, spleen, kidneys. He observes and recognizes urine, excrement, tears, saliva, blood vessels, grease, and observing and knowing them all, he is unattached and regrets nothing. This is the way the practitioner observes the body in order to realize peace and joy and be able to end unwholesome thoughts and remove anxiety and sorrow.

"Further the practitioner meditates on this body in order to see the Four Elements of earth, water, fire, and air, and he distinguishes these Four Elements. Just like a skillful butcher or his apprentice might lay out the different parts of a slaughtered cow and distinguish the leg, heart, torso, and head, the practitioner observing his own body distinguishes the Four Elements just as clearly, seeing that this is earth, this is water, this is fire, and this is air. Thus the practitioner meditates on the body in the body in order to end attachment.

"Further, bhikkhus, one should observe this body as having many openings from which many impure substances flow. Just as we look at bamboo or reeds and see the joints in the canes, so the practitioner observes the body with many openings from which impure substances flow.

"Further, bhikkhus, the practitioner meditates on the corpse of one who has died one day ago or one week ago. It is distended, fetid, impure. Then he meditates on his own body and sees that his own body is no different. This very body of his will not be able to escape death. The practitioner observes this corpse being seen and pecked at by vultures, being discovered and gnawed at by all sorts of wild creatures like tigers, panthers, and wolves, and then comes back to observing his own body and sees that it is no different. 'This very body of mine will not be able to escape that condition.' This is how the practitioner meditates on the body to realize peace and joy.

"Further, bhikkhus, the practitioner visualizes a corpse, which has lain on the ground for a year. It is half-eaten, fetid, and impure. Then he comes back to meditating on his own body and sees that his own body is no different. 'This very body of mine will not be able to escape that condition.' This is how the practitioner meditates on the body.

"Further, bhikkhus, the practitioner visualizes the corpse from which the skin and flesh has shriveled away. All that is left are the bones stained with blood. Then he comes back to meditating on his own body and sees that his own body is no different. 'This very body of mine will not be able to escape that condition.' This is how the practitioner meditates on the body.

"Further, bhikkhus, the practitioner visualizes a skeleton, which is just bones held together by some ligaments. Then he comes back to meditating on his own body and sees that his own body is no different. 'This very body of mine will not be able to escape that condition.' This is how the practitioner meditates on the body.

"Further, bhikkhus, the practitioner visualizes a corpse which has become a collection of scattered bones, all in different places: the hand bone, leg bone, ribs, shoulder blades, spinal column, kneecap, and skull. Then he comes back to meditating on his own body and sees that his own body is no different. 'This very body of mine will not be able to escape that condition.' His body will also decay in that way. This is how the practitioner meditates on the body in order to realize peace and joy.

"Further, bhikkhus, the practitioner visualizes a corpse which has become a collection of bones bleached like shells. Then he comes back to meditating on his own body and sees that his own body is no different. 'This very body of mine will not be able to escape that condition.' His body will also decay in that way. This is how the practitioner meditates on the body.

"Further, bhikkhus, the practitioner visualizes a corpse which has become a collection of yellowing bones, to which there is nothing worth being attached, or bones that have become the color of ash and are no longer distinguishable from the earth. Thus the practitioner meditates on his own body, abandoning unwholesome thoughts and removing sorrow and anxiety, observing, 'This body is impermanent, it is something which decomposes.' A practitioner who observes himself like this from within or from without, or both from within and without the body together understands that there is nothing which is eternal."

III.

"How does the practitioner meditate on the feelings in the feelings?

"When the practitioner has a pleasant feeling, he knows that he has a pleasant feeling. When he has a painful feeling, he knows that he has a painful feeling. When his feelings are neutral, he knows that his feelings are neutral. When he has a pleasant, painful, or neutral feeling with a material basis, he knows that he has a pleasant, painful, or neutral feeling with a material basis. When he has a pleasant, painful, or neutral feeling with a nonmaterial basis, he knows he has a pleasant, painful, or neutral feeling with a nonmaterial basis. This is how the practitioner meditates on the feelings in the feelings by his own insight.

"Further, bhikkhus, when the practitioner has a pleasant feeling, then there is not a painful feeling, and the practitioner knows there is a pleasant feeling. When there is a painful feeling, then there is not a pleasant feeling, and the practitioner knows that there is a painful feeling. When there is a neutral feeling, then there is neither a pleasant feeling nor a painful feeling, and the practitioner is aware that the feeling is neither pleasant nor painful. The practitioner is aware of the arising of all dharmas and the disappearance of all dharmas in such a way that, by his own insight, he realizes peace and joy. As feelings arise, the practitioner recognizes and is aware of them and their roots, and he is not dependent on them and does not give rise to feelings of attachment to the world. At that time there is no fear, and having no fear, he liberates himself forever from illusion and realizes nirvana. Birth and death are no longer. The holy life has been lived. What needs to be done has been done. There will be no more rebirth. He understands this directly. This is how the practitioner is aware of the feelings in the feelings to end dispersed thinking and remove sorrow and anxiety. Such is the meditation on the inside of the feelings and the outside of the feelings."

IV.

"What is meant by meditating on the mind in the mind in order to realize peace and joy?

"When the practitioner has desire in his mind, he knows that he has desire in his mind. When he does not have desire, he knows that he does not have desire. When he has hatred in his mind, he knows that he has hatred in his mind. When he does not have hatred, he knows that he does not have hatred. When he has confusion in his mind, he knows that he has confusion in his mind. When he does not have confusion, he knows that he does not have confusion. When he has craving in his mind, he knows that he has craving in his mind. When he does not have craving, he knows that he does not have craving. When there is mastery of his mind, he knows that there is mastery of his mind. When there is no mastery, he knows there is no mastery. When there is dispersion, he knows that there is dispersion. When there is no dispersion, he knows that there is no dispersion. When there is inattention, he knows that there is inattention. When there is no inattention, he knows that there is no inattention. When there is universality, he knows that there is universality. When there is no universality, he knows that there is no universality. When there is extensiveness, he knows that there is extensiveness. When there is not extensiveness, he knows that there is not extensiveness. When there is boundlessness, he knows that there is boundlessness. When there is not boundlessness, he knows that there is not boundlessness. When there is concentration, he knows that there is concentration. When there is no concentration, he knows that there is no concentration. When he has not yet realized liberation, he knows that he has not yet realized liberation. When he has realized liberation, he knows that he has realized liberation.

"This is how the practitioner is mindful of the mind in the mind. He observes the arising of dharmas, observes the destruction of dharmas, or observes both the arising and destruction of dharmas; being mindful of dharmas in order to realize peace and joy. He is able to see, know, and observe what is not observable, and he does not become dependent on the object and does not give rise to worldly thoughts. Because there are no thoughts of attachment to the world, there is no fear. Because there is no fear, there is no residue of affliction. When there is no residue of affliction, nirvana arises, and birth and death are no more, the holy life is realized, what needs to be done has been done, and there will be no more rebirth. The practitioner knows all this to be true. Thus in his own person the practitioner observes mind in mind, both from within and from without, in order to remove uncontrolled thought and cut off all anxiety."

V.

"What is meant by 'meditating on the objects of mind in the objects of mind?'

"When the practitioner practices the first factor of awakening, mindfulness, it is in reliance on the initial application of thought, on no-craving, on destroying the unwholesome mind and abandoning the unwholesome dharmas. He practices the factors of awakening, investigation of dharmas, energy, joy, concentration, and letting go, in reliance on applied thought, in reliance on no-craving, in reliance on destroying the unwholesome dharmas. This is how he practices meditating on the objects of mind in the objects of mind.

"Further, bhikkhus, having been liberated from sensual attachment, having abandoned unwholesome dharmas, with initial application of thought and sustained thought, with joy, he delights to dwell in the first dhyana in order to have joy in his own person. This is how the practitioner meditates on the objects of mind in the objects of mind.

"Further, bhikkhus, with the passing of applied thought and sustained thought, a joy arises in his mind which leads to the oneness of mind. When there is no more initial application of thought and sustained thought, the practitioner, maintaining joy, enters the second dhyana that has peace as well as joy. This is how the practitioner meditates on the objects of mind in the objects of mind.

"Further, bhikkhus, with the passing of thought and the constant practice of letting go of applied thought, he enjoys for himself that state which the holy ones long for, where mindfulness in letting go is fully purified, and he enters the third dhyana. This is how the practitioner meditates on the objects of mind in the objects of mind.

"Further, bhikkhus, with the absence of joy, when anxiety about joy and elation as well as pleasure and pain are no longer, and his mindfulness in letting go is fully purified, he enters the fourth dhyana, and that is to meditate on the objects of mind in the objects of mind. He meditates on the arising of dharmas and the passing of dharmas in order to arrive at peace and joy. He realizes right mindfulness in the present moment. He is able to see, know, and abandon dispersion. He is no longer dependent on anything. He does not give rise to thoughts of the world. Because he does not have worldly thoughts, he is not afraid. When there is no fear, birth and death no longer exist, and the holy life has been accomplished, what needs to be done has been done, there is no more rebirth, and everything is known in its true nature."

VI.

"Bhikkhus, relying on this one way of entering the path, living beings are purified, freed from sorrow and anxiety, their minds no longer subject to agitation, their understanding stable, and they are able to realize nirvana. This one way in is the destruction of the Five Hindrances and practice of the Four Ways of Stopping and Concentrating the Mind." The bhikkhus who heard the Buddha teach thus, applied themselves joyfully at that time to the practice.

SUMMARY COMPARISON OF THE THREE VERSIONS

I.

This section is about the circumstances under which the sutra was delivered, the importance of the sutra, and the subject matter of the sutra, namely the Four Establishments of Mindfulness.

In the first and second versions, it says that the sutra was delivered at Kammassadhamma, in the land of the Kuru people. The third version says that the sutra was delivered in Jetavana Monastery in Sravasti.

In this section, all three versions use the term, "ekayana" (the One Vehicle). The third version uses this term in the title of the sutra.

The first and second versions use the term, "nian chu" (Establishments of Mindfulness) in the title.

A literal translation of the first sentence following the description of the location in the first version of the sutra would say, "This one way, O bhikkhus, is the way" or "This only way, O bhikkhus, is the way." (*ekayano ayam bhikkhave maggam*). The second version says, "O bhikkhus, there is a way." The third version says, "There is the 'one way in.' Why should it be called 'one way?' Because it refers to our single-mind concentration."

The first section of the first version is short and concise. The second version adds that all the Tathagatas of the three times, thanks to their practice of the Four Establishments of Mindfulness, were able to overcome the Five Obstacles and realize the path. The third version also mentions the Five Obstacles and says what they are. It also says that the Noble Eightfold Path is a path for practicing the Four Establishments of Mindfulness. In The One Way In Sutra, the Four Establishments of Mindfulness are called the "Four Practices to Stop and Concentrate the Mind." As previously discussed, there is some question whether the translator of the third version is Gautama Sanghadeva or Dharmanandi. If the translator had been Sanghadeva, it is likely he would have used the term "Four Establishments of Mindfulness," as he did in version two.

II.

This section expounds the ways of observing the body in the body. In the first version, six ways of observing the body are taught:
1. Observing the breathing
2. Observing the positions of the body
3. Observing movements and functions of the body
4. Observing the parts of the body
5. Observing the elements in the body
6. Observing a corpse

In the second version, these six ways of observing the body are also taught, but breathing is offered third following the positions and functions of the body. In the observation of a corpse, only five parts are given to this observation instead of the nine in the first version.

The third version teaches only three ways of observing the body. It does not include observing the breathing, the positions, or the functions of the body. There are eight parts to the meditation on observing a corpse.

The unique feature of the second version is that, after the six teachings on how to observe the movements and functions of the body, there is a section that deals with unwholesome thoughts. This section has two parts: how to use a wholesome mind to deal with an unwholesome mind and how to use the mind to restrain the mind, like a strong wrestler holding down a weak man. Both of these ideas come from Vitakkasanthana Sutta (Majjhima Nikaya 20). We can say with certainty that this part was added at a later date, and in fact was added in an inappropriate place in the sutra, because at this point, the Buddha is discussing the practice of observing the body in the body and has not yet reached the Establishment of Mind.

Other differences in the second version are teachings on the kind of concentration that gives birth to joy and happiness, which is equivalent to the first jhana, and a concentration that abandons joy but maintains happiness, which is equivalent to the second jhana, as well as meditations on purity, clear light, and signs. All this is evidence that the practice of the Four Jhanas had already begun to infiltrate the Sutra Pitaka, although discreetly. By the time of the third version, the practice of the jhanas is mentioned quite openly, by name. The meditation which observes the clear light can be seen as announcing the first steps in the formation of Pure Land Buddhism, and the meditation on the sign will be developed in the use of the kasina, a symbolic image visualized as a point of concentration.

When it comes to the section that teaches observing mindfully the different elements which constitute the body, the second version mentions six elements as opposed to the usual four elements of the first and third versions. The six elements are earth, water, air, fire, emptiness, and consciousness.

The third version has an additional practice that is the observation of impure elements pouring out from the apertures of the body (not as a part of the Nine Contemplations of the corpse).

In the third version, the phrase most often repeated is, "to arrive at peace and joy." The equivalent phrases most repeated in the first and second versions are as follows:

Version One:
> This is how a practitioner observes the body in the body. He observes the body from within or from without, or from both within and without. He observes the process of coming-to-be in the body or the process of dissolution in the body or both the process of coming-to-be and the process of dissolution. Or he is mindful of the fact, 'There is a body here,' until understanding and full awareness come about. He maintains the observation, free, not caught up in any worldly consideration. That is how to practice observation of the body in the body.

Version Two:
> This is how the practitioner is aware of body as body, both inside the body and outside the body, and establishes mindfulness

in the body with recognition, insight, clarity, and realization. This is called being aware of body as body.

These paragraphs are repeated in the sections of the sutra teaching observation of the feelings, the mind, and the dharmas, substituting the words feelings, mind, or dharmas for the word body. If we are bothered by questions such as "How can there be an inside of the feelings or an outside of the feelings?" when we read, "mindfully observing the feelings in the feelings, observation of the feelings from within or from without, or from both within and without," we must remember that repetition, though not always relevant, is a mark of oral transmission. The second version uses the phrase, "observes the body as the body" (Chinese: *guan shen ru shen*) instead of the phrase, "observes the body in the body" (Pali: *kaye kayanupassana*).

III.

This section concerns the practice of observing the feelings in the feelings. "Feelings" is the translation from the Pali vedana in the first version. In the second version the Chinese word used to translate vedana is *jue,* while in the third version the word used is *tong.* Why does the third version use tong instead of jue? The original meaning of tong is "painful." Perhaps the translator had been strongly influenced by the doctrine that every single feeling is suffering. In this third section, the third version emphasizes that when there is a painful feeling, there cannot be a pleasant feeling, and when there is a pleasant feeling, there cannot be a painful feeling. It also emphasizes the necessity of observing mindfully the arising and disappearing of feelings and knowing their source in order not to be imprisoned in them or afraid of them. This is a positive point in the third version.

The following is a quotation from the third version: "Because he is not afraid, he is able to realize nirvana. Birth and death are no more, the holy life has been realized, what needs to be done has been done, there will be no more births." This quotation, which is not found in the first and second versions, appears three times in the third version. It is a sentence that is found over and over again in the sutras and most probably during the course of oral transmission it was added here.

IV.

This section deals with observing the mind in the mind. The third version does not mention mindfulness of the process of the arising and disappearing of psychological phenomena as do the first and second versions. In the third version, it is mentioned that we observe the dharmas that we can know, see, and observe as well as dharmas that we cannot observe. The word "observe" here has the meaning of practicing mindful observation. Observing dharmas which cannot be observed is a strange idea, equivalent to the teaching of the Sutra of Forty-Two Chapters, "Our practice is the practice which is non-practice," which has a strong Mahayana flavor.

An additional quotation of interest from the third version is: "The practitioner does not rely on anything at all, does not give rise to thoughts of the world. Because there is no arising of such thoughts, there is no more fear. Because there is no more fear, no residue of the afflictions is left, and nirvana is realized." The latter part of this quotation is nearly equivalent to the Prajñaparamita Hrdaya Sutra: "Having no obstacles, they overcome fear, liberating themselves forever from illusion and realizing perfect nirvana."

V.

This part deals with the practice of observing dharmas in dharmas. In the first version, we have the practices of observing the Five Obstacles, the Five Skandhas, the Twelve Realms of Sense Organs and Sense Objects, the Seven Factors of Awakening, and the Four Noble Truths. The first version (in its form in the Digha Nikaya) develops a teaching on the mindful observation of the Four Noble Truths and the Noble Eightfold Path, and this development is what gives it its name Maha ("great") Satipatthana. The second version only teaches mindful observation of the Twelve Realms, the Five Obstacles, and the Seven Factors of Awakening.

The third version only teaches the Seven Factors of Awakening. (It has already dealt with the Five Obstacles in its first section.) Possibly because of carelessness on the part of the copyist, only six of the Seven Factors of Awakening are mentioned: mindfulness, investigation of dharmas, energy, joy, concentration, and equanimity. The third version teaches the Four Jhanas. The terms *vitarka* and *vicara*, usually translated as "initial application" and "sustained attention" are translated into Chinese as *jue* ("perception") and *guan* ("observation"). In this fifth section, the third version repeats the phrases we have already seen in the second and fourth sections and which have been compared with part of the Prajñaparamita Hrdaya Sutra, and adds some words that make it seem even closer to the Prajñaparamita. These words are equivalent to "liberating themselves forever from illusion" of the Prajñaparamita.

VI.

This section deals with the length of time the practitioner needs to realize the fruits of the practice, and it identifies what those fruits are. The first version says that the fruit known as the highest understanding can be reached in this very life, if the practitioner practices the

Establishments of Mindfulness. The sutra says that practicing for seven years, five years, down to one month, and half a month, and, finally, seven days, can also result in the highest understanding.

The second version goes farther, saying that to practice mindfulness for one day and night can lead to highest awakening, or that if we begin to practice in the morning, by the afternoon the practice will already have results. The third version does not mention the period of time necessary for realizing the fruits of the practice.

Parallax Press, a nonprofit organization, publishes books on engaged Buddhism and the practice of mindfulness by Thich Nhat Hanh and other authors. All of Thich Nhat Hanh's work is available at our online store and in our free catalog. For a copy of the catalog, please contact:

Parallax Press
www.parallax.org
P.O. Box 7355
Berkeley, CA 94707
Tel: (510)525-0101

Individuals, couples, and families are invited to practice the art of mindful living in the tradition of Thich Nhat Hanh at retreat communities in France and the United States. For information, please visit www.plumvillage.org or contact:

Plum Village
13 Martineau
33580 Dieulivol, France
info@plumvillage.org

Green Mountain Dharma Center
P.O. Box 182
Hartland Four Corners, VT 05049
mfmaster@vermontel.net
Tel: (802)436-1103

Deer Park Monastery
2499 Melru Lane
Escondido, CA 92026
deerpark@plumvillage.org
Tel: (760)291-1003

For a worldwide directory of Sanghas practicing in the tradition of Thich Nhat Hanh, please visit www.iamhome.org.

Back Cover Material

BUDDHISM/SPIRITUALITY

"If you were to possess only one book on how to fare through this human existence with joy and self-knowledge, it should be this text."

—*Karuna* Magazine

Transformation & Healing presents one of the Buddha's most fundamental teachings and the foundation of all mindfulness practice. The Sutra on the Four Establishments of Mindfulness has been studied, practiced, and handed down with special care from generation to generation for 2,500 years. This sutra teaches us how to deal with anger and jealousy, to nurture the best qualities in our children, spouses, and friends, and to greet death with compassion and equanimity.

Thich Nhat Hanh's commentary is organized into twenty exercises that guide readers through the fundamentals of Buddhist practice and offer insights into mindfulness in daily life.

Thich Nhat Hanh is a Vietnamese Zen Master, poet, scholar, and human rights activist. In 1967, he was nominated by Martin Luther King, Jr. for the Nobel Peace Prize. He is the author of more than one hundred books, including *Being Peace, Old Path White Clouds*, and *Calming the Fearful Mind*. He lives at Plum Village, his meditation center in France, and travels worldwide, leading retreats on the art of mindful living.

www.ingramcontent.com/pod-product-compliance
Lightning Source LLC
Chambersburg PA
CBHW011750220426
43670CB00019B/2932